"Josh Moody is absolutely correct in [...] a model for engaging Enlightenment [...] what the Edwards model would mean [...] church are potent, thoughtful, and constructive. This is a book that is sure to start many profitable conversations."

R. ALBERT MOHLER, JR.
President, The Southern Baptist Theological Seminary

"Josh Moody convincingly demonstrates the transcendent applicability of Jonathan Edwards' theo-centric, biblio-centric, and cardio-centric theology to both the church and the world of our day. The God-Centered Life is a graced prescription for truly engaging today's culture —as Edwards did in his day. This is a bracing, energizing read!"

R. KENT HUGHES
Senior Pastor Emeritus, College Church in Wheaton

"For the sagging programmatic and pragmatic efforts that so characterize North American congregations, Moody's work offers an invitation to re-focus on the God-centered life. I heartily commend this work as a timely and valuable resource."

DAVID S. DOCKERY
President, Union University

"At last someone who stands in the tradition of Edwards as a pastor-scholar interpreting and applying the lessons from Jonathan Edwards for today. A realistic, pastorally sensitive, yet academically based application of Puritan thinking to the key issues of revival, religious experience, modernity, leadership and family life. Josh Moody embodies intelligent insight from the pulpit, counseling room, library in bringing Edwards alive and speak very directly to topics ranging from New Christian Movements to the failures of Christian leaders. A thoughtful, worthwhile read."

E. DAVID COOK
Holmes Professor, Wheaton College
Fellow, Green College, Oxford

"I recommend this book most highly, praying that Josh Moody's labors will encourage the kinds of 'Edwards influenced' lives and congregations that our world so desperately needs. Edwards' God-centered life can inspire us all to greater faithfulness, whether or not we affirm every detail of his doctrine. His passions for the gospel and the spread of the kingdom of God have much to teach us in the twenty-first century."

DOUGLAS A. SWEENEY
Associate Professor of Church History,
Trinity Evangelical Divinity School

"With a sure grasp of the details of Jonathan Edwards' life and the deep structures of his thought, as well as a keen understanding of today's church scene, Josh Moody is well placed to show where, and where not, Edwards should be heeded. Powerfully challenging and highly recommended."

MICHAEL HAYKIN,
Principal and Professor, Toronto Baptist Seminary

"The God-Centered Life accomplishes a rare feat for a Jonathan Edwards scholar: reaching down without dumbing down. Here you will find why and how Jonathan Edwards' message, ministry, and even mistakes are relevant and thus sorely needed for contemporary Christians. Discussions as wide-ranging as Enlightenment epistemological shifts and postmodern breakdown of families all converge on how Edwards might figure in these key intellectual and existential issues of great import today.

PAUL LIM
Assistant Professor of the History of Christianity
Vanderbilt University

"I feel that the insights here are ones the church today needs to apply. Church leaders: read this book! It's accessible in style and deep in content. Don't miss it!"

STEPHEN GAUKROGER
Senior Pastor, Gold Hill Baptist Church, Buckinghamshire, England

THE GOD-CENTERED LIFE

THE GOD-CENTERED LIFE

Insights from Jonathan Edwards for Today

JOSH MOODY

REGENT COLLEGE PUBLISHING
Vancouver, British Columbia

First published 2006 in the UK by
InterVarsity Press
38 De Montfort Street, Leicester LE1 7GP, England
Website: www.ivpbooks.com
Email: ivp@ivp-editorial.co.uk

This edition published 2007 by
Regent College Publishing
5800 University Boulevard
Vancouver, BC V6T 2E4 Canada
Website: www.regentpublishing.com

Library and Archives Canada Cataloguing in Publication

Moody, Josh
The God-centered life : insights from Jonathan Edwards for today /
Josh Moody.

Includes bibliographical references.
ISBN-10: 1-57383-386-X
ISBN-13: 978-1-57383-386-8

1. Edwards, Jonathan, 1703-1758. 2. Christian life. I. Title.

BX7260.E3M66 2006   230'.58092   C2006-904747-2

CONTENTS

FOREWORD

This is a book for anyone concerned about the health of the contemporary evangelical church, or indeed for the future of biblical Christianity, in our secular Western culture. There is no doubt that the challenges we face are massive, if there is ever to be a substantial change in the spiritual climate of the "developed" world. Our intellectual non-engagement with postmodernism, the unreality of so much that passes as "doing church," the sheer incredibility of the Christian world-view – all of this and much more constitutes the daily experience of today's Christian "mountaineers," who really want to make a difference for God in daily life. It is like climbing a precipitous rock face, and it can often be paralyzing. Yet we have a God who not only empowers climbers, but can also move mountains. As the title implies, our biggest problem is that we are centered on ourselves, rather than on God, which is why we find it so hard to imagine that things could ever be different. We need a radical realignment of our thinking and our living, and it is the genius of this engaging study that Josh Moody uses the eighteenth-century New England Puritan scholar-pastor, Jonathan Edwards, as his catalyst. Having carried out his doctoral research on Edwards' life and ministry, Dr. Moody is a sure guide to the heart and mind of a man who has been called the greatest American theologian, and by some her greatest philosopher. Here you will find church history at its very best – detailed research, scholarly insight, pithy quotations, mature judgment – but always in the service of the contemporary church and the issues we are currently facing. For Moody's thesis is that Edwards also faced a shifting of the cultural tectonic plates in his own generation, so that he provides us with an enormously relevant and helpful model of how to respond biblically in a similar context. Not that Edwards is the focus of the book. This is not hagiography. But the immense spiritual and intellectual stature of the man and the powerful continuing influence of his life and works show us how true God-centeredness revolutionizes Christian ministry and eventually can even change cultures. In Edwards we see a man, totally submitted to the authority of Scripture (as we must be), but, as Josh Moody points out, without that becoming "a prison to his mind." His biblical intelligence fed and informed his faith, just as his faith enabled him to think straight about the challenges he faced, whether from the growing scientific skepticism, or from the fanaticism of revivalist enthusiasts, to name but two. Like his mentor, Josh Moody exhibits the strengths of both scholar and pastor. I have known him since his days in student leadership in Cambridge and rejoice to see the flourishing of his ministry in New Haven, with his involvement at Yale. There is much to help us here, as through Edwards' lens, we refocus biblical ministry priorities for today. The rehabilitation of the biblical concept and definition of revival, the relationship and interaction of reason and faith, the poverty of so much modern preaching, the criteria by which spiritual reality can be recognized and assessed, the principle of biblical intelligence – all these are areas carefully explored, with wise insight and penetrating applications to our current situation. But none of this is dusty or remote. I came away from each chapter informed, challenged and above all renewed and refreshed in my dependence upon the God of the Word, whom Edwards knew, loved and served so uncompromisingly, but so humanly as well. We are greatly indebted to Josh Moody for producing a quality historical account that is so accessible and engaging, but then using it to speak with such help to our day and especially to the priorities of our Christian lives, in the church and in the world. It moves us to thank God for Jonathan Edwards, who still speaks so powerfully, but above all to worship and adore his God and ours.

DAVID JACKMAN
President, Proclamation Trust
London, February 2006

PREFACE

I suspect that for many of us, our Christian experience is too often influenced by our circumstances. When we are "up," God is great. When we are "down," God is distant. If things go our way, we have much for which to praise God. If times come that would test the patience of Job, we are tempted to give up.

I have taken the time to write this book because the great message of the Bible is one that is *God*-centered, not *us*-centered or *me*-centered. This makes all the difference. God always comes first. He is always at the heart of life. He influences and invades all of reality. He *is*, and there is no other. Why does this make all the difference? Because then my happiness is not dependent on my personal experience, but on God's grace and love for me. Of course, this is the very heart of the gospel. While we were still sinners, Christ died for us. His love is not dependent on our moral performance, but on his divine affection. It was God in Christ who was reconciling the world to himself. It is not only the heart of the gospel, it is also the very core of what it means to become a Christian at all. We are "born from above," of the Spirit, we repent and we have faith in Christ. We undergo a revolution of the heart whereby our core being is altered; changed from being centered on the self, however nice or clean that self may be, to being centered on God. What is more, this God-centeredness is not only at the very heart of our faith, it is also the element of the Christian message most likely to be missed in our day. If the contemporary West is anything, it is individualistic, centered on answering the great question, "What's in it for me?" So this matter of being God-centered needs to be trumpeted from our pulpits. We need constantly to reorientate ourselves around God and his Word, lest our vision and purpose become subtly influenced by the market, or trendy humanistic moral sensibilities. It really is urgent. And surprisingly, for something so contemporary, I have found that significant help in this area comes from one Jonathan Edwards, a pastor-teacher from a bygone era, whose work, life and writings witness particularly to the foundational reality of a God-centered life.

In writing a book like this, you pick up a burden of gratitude to many. I wish heartily to thank IVP for their sterling work on this project, and in particular my editor Philip Duce for his painstaking expertise; it truly has been a privilege to work with him, as with Rob Clements of Regent who expertly edited the American version of this book. My thanks also go to David Jackman for his foreword. David has been of profound encouragement to many of us down through the years and we will be glad if we can follow his example of faithful and effective service for our Lord. I am very grateful to Michael Haykin for his warm commendation, as well as to Stephen Gaukroger whose ministry is an inspiration. Similarly my gratitude extends to R. Albert Mohler, Jr., R. Kent Hughes, David S. Dockery, Douglas A. Sweeney, E. David Cook, and Paul Lim for their commendations. It is usual also to extend thanks to family and church for their support, but my gratitude goes beyond tradition. Thank you, Rochelle, for your tireless support as my wife and for the ministry to which God has called us. Josiah and Sophia: may you always grow to be increasingly God-Centered; thank you for sharing me with the church. Don Kim read an early draft and gave helpful critique and input. David Schwaderer has been invaluable in putting together the American edition. Sherrie Morrison has helped, as always, in various administrative matters, often beyond the call of duty. I am grateful for the ministry team at the church here of staff, our associate pastor Jay Ridenour for his most fruitful ministry, elders and deacons, and for the warm fellowship of the whole body. Mark Dever's personal encouragement and teaching have been invaluable to me. Don Carson's example of intellectually credible biblical exposition has often functioned as water in a parched land. Pat Blake has been a much appreciated, faithful, wise friend and counselor over the years, as have my parents and family, and other good brothers and sisters in the faith. As we think of all those who help and encourage us (and there are many others I could list who have prayed for me, taught me, supported me in one way or another), we, who aim to be God-centered, are moved to consider him to whom we render all thanks and praise, and from whom, we hope in all grace, to receive the Master's commendation on that day: "Well done, good and faithful servant!" (Matthew 25:23).

JOSH MOODY
Trinity Baptist Church
New Haven, CT

1.

JONATHAN EDWARDS
IN OUR TIMES

It was a church like any other. The denomination does not matter. The music was fine, even stately. The preaching was sane, perhaps inspiring. The people were nice, neatly authentic. And at the end of the service there was coffee.

After the coffee everyone left to go their separate ways. I was left to wonder, 'Is this it?' Does this pleasant rendition of religion amount to the vision cast by our Lord for the New Testament Church? Would it have been better if there had been more miracles? What if the sermon had plumbed greater depths? How about if the music had been more technically skilled? What if the people had stayed for a few more minutes to converse?

If my experience of church is anything like yours – and, again, the denomination is immaterial – I suspect it does not so much leave a bitter taste in your mouth as a timid feeling of having missed something. Did God show up and we did not notice?

The church today is in rude health by many statistics. In America at least, the size of congregations, their budgets, their buildings and their political influence is as never before. In parts of the developing world numerical growth in church attendance is outpacing all predictions.

In Britain, where I am from, and Europe the statistics are not so rosy, but Bible-believing Christians are a growing force. But peek beneath the surface even in America and you discover worrying trends. J.I. Packer once described religion in America as a thousand miles wide and one inch deep. Evangelical statistician George Barna estimates that basic moral behavior is no different among America's many church attendees from their secular counterparts. The divorce rate is the same and petty theft at work is the same. While the innocence of the new churches in the rest of the world is appealing, its massive growth prompted John Stott to comment that the greatest problem of the contemporary church is "growth without maturity." Teaching and discipleship are needed as never before.

With this strange paradox of the contemporary church, boom and bust at once, wealth and spiritual poverty combined, we need to wrestle and, like Jacob, overcome. I contend that Jonathan Edwards provides us with a model of Christian faithfulness that it will serve us well to emulate.

A PERSONAL ODYSSEY

I first began to realize Jonathan Edwards' timeliness as I was meandering down the narrow book-lined "stacks" in the main library at Cambridge University. I was thinking intently as I wandered along those book-shelves. My memory of that mental process is razor sharp even now, years later. My mind was focused on solving the problem of answering the challenge modern philosophy and science had posed Christianity. I had learnt that the roots of this challenge lay in the historical period of the Enlightenment. And, as I stumbled along, my mind was searching for a voice speaking in the age of the Enlightenment who had not only spotted the direction of its non-Christian movement at its earliest stage, but who also ably counteracted it.

Head in the clouds, mind on cerebral matters, I skirted stack after stack thinking, pondering. I'm one of those people who occasionally generates such all-consuming mental pictures that the outside world momentarily fades from view. My wife can find this maddening. "Hello, dear!" she will say. "Did you hear what I said?" But when my mind is on planet intellectual it takes interstellar space travel to get it down to earth. I was thinking. I even remember I was doing some praying too.

I turned down one of the stacks and pulled out a book at random, a large hard-covered book. The sort you can use as a doorstop when not reading.

I picked it up, flicked open a page, the first page that my thumb happened upon. The one I came to was a drawing of a spider flying through the air, or at least of how they apparently do that. It was a rather technical early scientific kind of drawing. Interesting, I thought. I checked the date. The author lived from 1703 to 1758, which meant he was around at the beginning of the Enlightenment.

Americans, of course, are familiar with Jonathan Edwards. They have read one of his sermons during high school. On the other side of the Atlantic from them, however, Jonathan Edwards does not even appear as a blip on the cultural radar screen.

Intrigued, I put the volume back and picked out another by the same author. This was equally large and impressive-looking. I began to read and found the pages packed with expositions of biblical texts. They were classic Puritan sermons, with the Puritan preaching style and the kinds of phrases Puritans loved to use.

I stopped suddenly. *Hold on,* I thought, *I've just read what appears to be a very early Newton-like piece of scientific investigation. Now, by the same author, I've read a Puritan sermon. This could be it.*

Steadily I devoured from cover to cover the two volumes of the *Works of Edwards* (Banner of Truth, 1988). The typeface in these volumes is tiny. I was already short-sighted, but poring over Edwards' words in such small print may well have increased my glasses' prescription strength. I began to live and work in the former Soviet Union republic of Georgia as a missionary. At that stage in the nation's history there were more bombs than bonuses – it was just after the civil war. So my experience of reading Edwards deeply for the first time is inescapably associated with hearing machine-gun fire in the old city of Tbilisi; as I was later to learn, Edwards himself lived close to the frontier, with less sophisticated military hardware but comparable instability. I read on and on. There wasn't much else by way of reading matter. I took with me a backpack full of clothes and the two Edwards volumes sandwiched between my socks.

Increasingly I thought of doing a PhD in theology. I settled on Edwards for my thesis and Cambridge University as my alma mater once more. I had already read just about everything published by Edwards, so now I consumed everything even vaguely related to the subject. I began to make connections. Eventually I ended up finding in Edwards' work answers to many of the questions that bugged me. How could I know God genuinely? How could I proclaim this God in a secular society? How could I explain spiritual experience to people who equated God with a New Age force? Time and again Edwards' reflections on Scripture delivered.

As part of my doctorate research I was a visiting scholar at Yale University. Yale houses the world's largest selection of Edwards' manuscripts in the Beinecke Library. This center is the "Mecca" of Edwards studies and I spent many a happy hour laboring at Edwards' impossibly spidery handwriting. Now, in God's sovereignty, I am the pastor of a church within walking distance of Yale campus.

In my view Jonathan Edwards is not merely an historical figure. Obviously Edwards occupied a slice of history some three hundred years ago. We need to be sensitive to these historical realities in order to avoid making Edwards in our own image. If we are to understand Edwards at all, we must understand him on his own terms. He was an eighteenth-century person, a Puritan pastor, a man who lived in colonial America and whose attitude and actions were shaped by that historical context.

Nonetheless, because Edwards was forming a foundational response to the Enlightenment, his basic message is particularly timely today. Our society has also created a reaction to the Enlightenment heritage of modern rationalism and empirical science. We are increasingly wary of absolutes. Certainty is suspect. It reminds us of the rational "totalitarianism" that produced ideologies that bled the twentieth century. We are also fearful of more primitive absolute religious instincts. We may feel that when they are not framed in Christian love they can create terrorist activities. We are not tempted to go back to a pre-Enlighten-ment age of religious certainty. Nor are we attracted by the Enlighten-ment modernity that saw creedal certainty vested in the human senses and the human mind. Instead we look to a future without absolutes at all. As Bill Clinton said in a public lecture at Yale University, "Anyone who believes in absolute truth is just wrong." Clinton was apparently unaware of the self-contradiction involved in an absolute denial of absolutes, as was most of his audience, who instead were, as many of us are today, attracted by a vision of global peace without doctrinal divisions.

This idealistic vision of the future is as much a mirage as the views of those post-Second World War utopians who predicted a working week of four days, or the Internet geeks who touted an end to the economic cycle in the wired world. Edwards helps us see why this is the case, what to do about it, and what alternative vision should be held up before the minds of Christian people.

THE LAY OF THE LAND

Some perspective will help. Here are four other current approaches to interpreting Edwards.

First there is the "Yale School" on Edwards. The Yale School is the dominant scholarly consensus. This is for the very good reason that the Yale Jonathan Edwards Project has done much of the coalface work on the actual Edwards manuscripts. Within what we may broadly describe as the Yale School, there are several different strands of interpretation. There are those who are sympathetic to Edwards' beliefs and do their work on Edwards with warm Christian piety. Less recently, others, more in line with the old Perry Miller idea that Edwards was a genius unfortunately bound by Christian doctrine, appreciated Edwards' phi-losophy, aesthetics and intelligence, but not his faith. In general terms, though, the Yale School's approach is that Edwards is best understood on his own terms as an early eighteenth-century Puritan preacher and pastor.

Second, the American pastor John Piper has based much of his popular preaching upon a passionate appreciation of Edwards' theology. Piper knows his history and understands the cultural context in which Edwards worked, but his emphasis is more upon Edwards' experiential Christianity. Piper's dominant theme, "God is most glorified in us when we are most satisfied in him," is taken out of the genetic heritage of Edwards and grafted into contemporary preaching, evangelism and church. The successful ministry of John Piper is a testimony to Edwards' enduring significance. In some ways a great introduction to Edwards is John Piper's book *Desiring God* (Multnomah, 2003).

Third is what we could refer to as the "Banner School" on Edwards, meaning the publishers of Edwards' *Works*, Banner of Truth. The Banner School is in many ways similar to Piper's approach, except it accents Edwards more as a defender of true revival. Edwards is described as the proponent of God-centered revival, not of "revivalism," which the second Great Awakening (in the nineteenth century) turned into a kind of machine that people thought they could crank into operation with the right techniques.

Fourth is also an amalgamation of approaches to Edwards whereby Edwards' descriptions of revivals are garnered for similarities to contemporary supernatural experiences of the Spirit, and used as apologetic support for those experiences. Perhaps for shorthand we could call this the "Blessing" reading of Edwards.

Each of these has something to say. It is essential we have a firm grasp of the historical setting in which Edwards existed. Without that, any conclusions about the implications of his message will be forlorn – if not anachronistic. In this regard, the recent mushrooming of Edwards scholarship associated with the Jonathan Edwards Project at Yale has helped develop a fuller picture of Edwards in his times. It is also important to garner theological insights from Edwards, which the other three current approaches to Edwards all do, with varying conclusions.

In addition, though, it is vital to see that Edwards' message is timely to our age in a special way. Because he preached the historic Christian gospel, and because that gospel is still true today, Edwards' message, like that of any genuine Christian preacher, is relevant throughout the ages. But Edwards' contribution is particularly timely today because his great sparring partners, the Enlightenment and the secularist modernism it bequeathed, have defined the recent progression of our culture. Whereas Edwards was responding to the Enlightenment at the *beginning,* our culture has reacted to Enlightenment modernism at the *end.* If Edwards formed an effective and biblical response to the Enlightenment, we will have lots to learn from him.

There are many other more piecemeal things we can learn from him, though. Edwards was a great preacher: we can learn from that. Edwards was a godly man: we can learn from that. However, if we can digest the meat of his ministry and not just the seasoning, if we can learn from his response to the Enlightenment which informed both his preaching and his living, we will be aided in responding to our culture's reaction to the Enlightenment as well.

While we should not accord Edwards or any other teacher past or present the same level of attention as Holy Scripture itself, we need not be scared to find in Edwards or any other true teacher past or present helpful guides to the application of Scripture. Part of God's provision for the church is the gift of teachers (Ephesians 4:11). We find teachers in our contemporary churches. We also find them throughout church history, sometimes given at an hour of acute need to bring a message from God for the church's healing and help. There are many great teachers or "doctors" of the church, including such luminaries as St. Augustine, Martin Luther and John Owen.

Augustine assisted in defending the church's solid foundation of grace. Luther stood firm upon the message of the Bible, summarized in his famous declaration "Here I stand; I can do no other." John Owen, probably the greatest of British theologians, wrote and preached extensively on an astonishingly wide variety of subjects and bequeathed to later generations a treasure store of insight. Edwards is also one of these great historic teachers given to the church to help it interpret Scripture. He too came at a crucial turning point in the history of God's work. The waves of the Enlightenment were beginning to pound against the rock of the church. Few at the time fully understood the growing implications of the philosophy of the Enlightenment. Of those who did, fewer still managed to develop an approach that was both effective and solidly biblical.

The Puritans in America were amazed by a new movement spearheaded by the evangelist George Whitefield. In England the established Church of England struggled to accept, and indeed outright persecuted, the evangelical awakening led by Whitefield and Wesley. Missionaries were making great strides into the wilderness of America. There was activity everywhere, evangelistic, doctrinal and philosophical. Edwards stood at the apex of a new stage in the history of the Western world and pointed it in one direction. The main course of Western history has ignored him. As we lurch from intellectual crisis to moral redundancy, it is time to listen to Edwards.

The idea, then, is both to find Edwards in his times and to apply him to ours. The very possibility of learning contemporary lessons from a historical period is denied by many professional historians. As Christians we know the biblical historical books are not only a catalogue of historical events, but also an interpretation of those events from God's perspective. The biblical historical writers do not blush at drawing conclusions from the malevolence of an ancient king and his eventual shameful demise to God's righteous judgment. But for us to write history, claiming this sort of insight into its meaning, is replete with pitfalls. We do not have the divine insight given to the inspired authors of, say, 2 Kings or 1 Samuel. There have been numerous examples of people claiming to be able to "read history" for its meaning in an immature and sometimes frankly dangerous way. The first task of a dictator is to rewrite history because the interpretation of the past empowers the mandate of the future. Christians must not play those kinds of games.

However, neither should we view history purely from a human point of view. If God is Lord of history, as he is, and if God's will in the Bible has been revealed to us, which it has, then it is not a complex deduction that sinful behavior will be judged and the faithful saved. That does not make us the judge, nor give us the right to pontificate on the righteousness or otherwise of other people. It does give us a standard (the Bible) against which we may assess and apply our discovery about the past to our contemporary age. As Woody Allen quipped, "The reason why history repeats itself is because no-one listened the first time around." We need to listen to the past.

No-one has a perfect knowledge of the past or a perfect interpretation of Scripture. It is illogical, though, to gravitate from this commendable humility towards the past and the Bible to develop a cynical view of historical understanding or biblical meaning. That would be like saying because I cannot have a perfect knowledge of another person, I cannot have a meaningful relationship with my friends. A more sensible approach is to say because communication is difficult, I will need to listen carefully to my friends, be sure to check also that I am being properly understood, and not quickly assume that my meaning is as obvious as it seems to me. When I do so, I will find that I understand better and am gradually better understood. In principle the same is true of our fallible interpretations of the Bible and the past. God's Word is perfect, but our interpretation is not. As we develop skills of interpretation, and genuinely seek to hear God's voice in His Word, we will find that our perception of what God is saying is dependable. The past functions as a commentary upon the Bible: as we read the story of the past, we see how God's Word was ignored, believed, obeyed, and the implications of those responses to the Bible.

To read about the dead pastor Jonathan Edwards should not be an exercise of rearranging dry bones. Instead, a Christian should attempt to discern the work of the Spirit in Edwards' life, in line with biblical teaching, and also gratefully receive God's message through those who attempt to relate Edwards' works to our day.

My goal in this book is not a technical work on Edwards. With the Edwards tercentenary came a multitude of new scholarly works on Edwards. And a dedicated researcher can access my PhD thesis (published by University Press of America, 2005) on Edwards by inter-library loan from Cambridge University. That kind of historical graft is essential before drawing any conclusions; it is also spiritually unproductive unless it has some sort of message for our lives today. People read books about the past for contemporary reasons, even when that is purely personal aesthetic pleasure. My purpose here is to provide insights from Jonathan Edwards that will be useful for Christian life and ministry. I want to broadcast what Edwards would say if he walked into the average church today.

IS THAT JONATHAN EDWARDS SITTING IN MY PEW?

Edwards would be shocked by the sermon. Edwards' sermons were packed with theology and intricate analysis of biblical texts. They were also rather long. I can imagine Edwards leaning over to the person in the pew next to him after the sermon and saying, "Is it over already?" There is no virtue in long and bad sermons. On the other hand, only so much content can fit into a certain length of time. Edwards' sermons were not only far longer than the average in most churches; they were also considerably more rigorous than any sermon I have ever heard delivered. That does not mean his sermons were "intellectual." In fact Edwards rarely used technical theological jargon: his phrasing was often simple. It was the ideas he was communicating that were profound not the diction that was pretentious. The structure and phrasing of the sermons were quite traditional and straightforward. For example, Edwards would begin a sermon like this:

> Christ addresses these words to Peter upon occasion of his profess-ing his faith in him as the Son of God. Our Lord was inquiring of his disciples, whom men said that he was; not that he needed to be informed, but only to introduce and give occasion to what follows. They answer, that some said he was John the Baptist, and some Elias, and others Jeremias, or one of the prophets. When they had thus given an account whom others said he was, Christ asks them, whom they said he was? Simon Peter, whom we find always zealous and

forward, was the first to answer: he readily replied to the question, 'Thou art Christ, the Son of the living God.'

(From Edwards' sermon "A Divine and Supernatural Light," on Matthew 16:17)

The members of the church who received such sermons were not university professors or theological professionals. They were influenced by the hard life of the frontier, the quick money to be made and the ever-present dangers. Although Edwards' congregation would have contained some highly educated people, many had little education. Nonetheless, there are no reports of anyone finding Edwards' preaching boring. We are told of people clinging to the pillars in rapt attention, not of folk lolling asleep on the pew rail in front. Edwards' sermons were long, straightforward and biblically relentless. I suspect if a preacher these days began a sermon in the same vein as a typical Edwards address, many hearers would be mentally channel-surfing before the second paragraph! In seminaries preachers are trained to think of "relevance": do not merely explain the passage but also establish its contemporary significance. A typical seminary sermon on the same passage Edwards preached on in such an apparently boring manner might instead begin like this:

"Today we have films about 'magic'. We have TV shows about demons. There are computer games with hidden spells and curses. Our media in this way are merely reflecting a popular interest in spiritual themes. What is definitely not popular, though, is to say that a particular spirituality is the correct version, or that your god is the only God. Surprisingly enough, then, the passage in front of us this morning describes Jesus congratulating Peter for making an exclusive spiritual statement. Peter has realized that Jesus is far more than a mere prophet. He says that he is the Christ, the Son of the living God. You won't find that on TV."

Edwards' style is quite different. Is Edwards' manner of preaching commendable today? I think the answer is both yes and no. The answer is no because part of the reason why Edwards managed to sustain such an intense focus in his sermons is that his congregation was more bibli-cally literate than the average congregation in the West nowadays. The Puritan heritage, famous for its rigorous biblical training, was itself built upon the Reformation and its rediscovery of the Bible. The combined legacy of these two traditions produced a rich store of biblical knowledge that Edwards and his hearers possessed in common. We live in an age, instead, where many are ignorant of the basic message of the Bible and the predominant communication means is the video not the logos, sight not word. A contemporary preacher assumes that his hearers accept the relevance of the Bible at his and their peril.

However, I think the answer is also partly yes. Edwards' style was not merely traditional; it was principled, built upon an understanding of who we are, what preaching is, and how to communicate the gospel according to the Bible. We find this in Edwards' careful explanation of the text. He believed his calling as a preacher was not simply to evoke a positive response but to teach biblical truth and engage an appropriate response to that truth. We also find this in Edwards' use of imagery. His sermons possessed a visual quality due to the vibrant word pictures he interwove into the sentences. He spoke of the spiritual life in terms of the senses – of what we could hear, see and feel – because he believed spiritual encounter with God was akin to a sixth sense. There is no need to pop in a video of a nice sunset if you discover that spiritual engagement with God is spiritually seen.

A comparison of Edwards' sermons with contemporary sermonettes reveals the poverty, brevity and superficiality of much that passes for preaching today. Is our desire for relevance and having a good "hook" at the beginning of a sermon encouraging us to be less substantial in our ministry and thereby more empty-headed in our churches? Are we fishing or are we becoming fish?

The second thing I think Edwards would notice is the commercial nature of our churches. There are financial realities to church govern-ment, including such practicalities as balancing annual budgets, which in this world will always be with us. Churches have a structure that in some ways is not dissimilar from other "worldly" organizations such as not-for-profit charities or businesses. Nonetheless, there are substantial differences too – namely the power of the gospel and the teaching the Bible gives about church government, godliness and discipline. The word that comes to mind when I imagine Edwards attending a typical board meeting, or getting to know a church today, is "astonished."

Edwards was as aware of the necessity of practical organization for the healthy functioning of a church as any modern pastor. Edwards was no head-in-the-clouds ascetic. Some of his private letters record canny business deals where he bought and sold sheep. He went to considerable lengths to stock his own personal library, and his notebooks record an extensive concern for efficiency of endeavor. He was also inevitably immersed in the social and political realities of his age. However, what would undoubtedly have astonished Edwards was the extent to which contemporary churches may be influenced in their organizational approach as much by current business practices as by the teaching of the Bible. Edwards' church experience was self-consciously shaped by biblical teaching about the church. He was a Puritan, part of a Reformation movement that had sought to purify the church. Today many evangelicals think the Bible does not tell us anything about church government or church structure or "how to do church," but merely about the message of the gospel.

This attitude could not be further removed from Edwards' belief about the church. He was willing to risk being thrown out of his pulpit – and in the end was indeed expelled – because he insisted on obedience to a biblical norm of church practice. The conflict is called the "Communion Controversy" and was full of technical doctrinal distinctions. But the startling thing for many a Christian today about the Communion Controversy is that there was a controversy at all. We do not tend to think the Bible speaks clearly about church government or organization, and it is hard for us to imagine having a controversy of such heat about communion.

The way we "do church" today is informed not only by biblical principles of loving one another and prioritizing evangelism, but also by various prudential considerations gleaned from non-profit organizations, businesses and party political campaigns. Edwards would have found this hard to accept. This is not because he was a traditionalist. George Whitefield, the great evangelist, preached at Edwards' church and, during the sermon, Edwards was reported to have shed many a tear. George Whitefield was an ecclesiastical innovator; he preached in pulpits if they were open to him and in fields if they were not. Edwards himself initiated organizationally; he proposed a "concert of prayer," an international Christian commitment to pray for revival. He spoke warmly of the value of personal testimony in evoking spiritual awakening in others.

Yet for Edwards these were activities principally drawn from the pages of Scripture. He did not feel at liberty to do church by whatever means available. He thought he should preach the gospel according to the pattern of the New Testament. This is what his lengthy series of sermons published as a "History of the Work of Redemption" are all about. Edwards wanted to establish that his method of evangelism and revival was truly biblical. Many revivalists today would not feel it even necessary to attempt to establish that their techniques are based upon biblical teaching. What matters today is not exegesis, but numbers. How many people made professions? How much money was gathered? It is the bottom line of commercial realities applied to the spiritual realm that unconsciously dominates much of contemporary church life.

To take a more Edwards-like approach to contemporary church life is not to advocate turning the clocks back. It is to obey what the Bible teaches about how a church should function. Part of the reason why people say they like Jesus but not the church is because contemporary churches are patently commercial in their approach. When people say they do not want to be "religious," they often mean they do not want to be associated with an institution that appears in practice little different from other large conglomerates, even if it is selling Jesus and not soap. We need to listen to Edwards' more pure view of the church. We can be principled without being prudish and effective without being compromised, by being consciously biblical in how we proceed and not just in what we believe.

Edwards would see something in today's average church that would thrill him: the mission noticeboard. Even small churches have in their foyer posters of missionaries they are supporting from around the world. Edwards lived in a day when Protestant world mission was still in its infancy. David Brainerd, the great father of Protestant church missionary endeavors, became an example to many future missionaries through his diary, which Edwards edited and published. 'Brainerd's Diary' has functioned as an inspiration to pioneer missionaries down through the years and across the world. Brainerd modeled a wonderfully warm and fervent piety coupled with apostle-like determination to spread the gospel.

This kind of Protestant missionary trail-blazing for the gospel spread far and wide, influencing even the likes of William Carey and David Livingstone. Today, many previously non-Christian nations have a large Christian population. Perhaps Edwards would look at a map of Africa, Korea, South America or even China and wonder whether his dreams of the millennium were being fulfilled, even if in a way he had not expected. Much of Edwards' future horizon was filled with this sense of the growing expanse of the kingdom of God through the ministry of the church of God, which would bring about a millennial semi-paradise.

Now we come to another, more divisive, issue Edwards would notice if he walked into a variety of contemporary churches. Today there are charismatic evangelicals, conservative evangelicals, moderate evangelicals, Arminian evangelicals, Reformed evangelicals, and the list goes on. "Evangelical" has become such a broad category that the word 'evangelical' requires a prior adjective to give it significance. Protestant Christianity appears irretrievably split, for this evangelical division is merely a subdivision within other longer-existing fragmentations of the Reformation heritage. How would Edwards respond to this disunity? Would he be in favor of an evangelical ecumenicism? Or would he take a particular side in the Protestant debate? And if he would take sides, whose side would he be on?

That question is not as easy to answer as it may at first appear to those with no more than a passing familiarity with Edwards' thought. Edwards certainly was a Calvinist, but, as he said, he accepted this appellation only "for the sake of definition." Edwards was a Puritan but he was a supporter of a revival movement led by two Anglican ministers, George Whitefield and John Wesley. Edwards was a Congregationalist but when searching for a new job after his long tenure at Northampton he was open to the possibility of serving in a Presbyterian church in Scotland. Edwards consistently baptized infants, but after lengthy and circuitous consideration of the implications of infant baptism concluded that "these things about baptism [are] doubtful" (A. Chamberlain [ed.], *The Works of Jonathan Edwards* [Yale University Press, 2000], vol. 18, p. 130).

Part of the way to appreciate these apparently contradictory impulses is to understand that the tradition in which Edwards stood emphasized being not only "Reformed," but also always "reforming." So even when Edwards is at his most innovative – and much of Edwards' thinking sparkles with originality – he is not essentially betraying a tradition that insists that all be ultimately judged by Scripture and not by tradition. It was a high accolade of his peers that Edwards was viewed as a theologian who more than any other studied the Bible. Edwards viewed the Bible not as a mental prison but as a seminal agent of expansion and growth: it did not confine him; it released him.

How would Edwards analyze the major division in the contemporary Protestant church between charismatics and non-charismatics? He believed the supernatural gifts of the Spirit had ceased with the closing of the apostolic age and that claims to direct "impressions" from God were fanatical. Some of his unpublished sermons are bracing in this regard! Even his more well-known works (for instance, the *Religious Affections*) spend a great deal of time distinguishing the experience of someone who is powerfully undergoing the work of the Spirit from someone who is delusional. But this does not mean Edwards would side with an anti-supernatural party, for Edwards was also on the side of profound experience of God. In this regard he is quite like his great latter-day follower and fan of the Puritans, the late Dr. Martyn Lloyd-Jones, who was also an advocate of profound experience of the Spirit. Prophets of the Word seem to be able to speak from the wilderness and challenge us all.

If Edwards not only listened to a contemporary sermon but also paid a visit to a contemporary university, one further distinction would arrest him: the separation of the intellectual and the scientific from the ecclesiastical and the spiritual. Churches tend to have activists as their leaders, and universities rarely have spiritually-minded presidents. Even at the individual level, it is rare today to find someone who is both a spiritual leader and an intellectual, both an activist and a philosopher, both an ideas person and an administrator. One of the reasons for this separation of the life of the mind from the life of the spirit is that modern society in general is far more specialized and complex. It is not really possible any more to be an expert in widely different fields of endeavor. More normally, a person's specialty is limited to a subfield of a discipline: you are not just a scholar, but you are a historian or a chemist; you are not a chemist, but you are a biochemist, and so on.

Apart from living in a less specialized society, Edwards' expansive reach as an intellectual and Christian leader was also made possible by his remarkable intelligence. He was a Mozart of theology, a child prodigy who went on to perform masterpieces. Edwards became an undergraduate at Yale College at 13, began his MA at 17, and was a tutor at Yale at 21. Before dying of a smallpox inoculation at 55, he became briefly President of Princeton. In between he was a preacher and pastor and a missionary to Native Americans, wrote numerous books, and was instrumental in the international revival known as the "Great Awakening." That combination of activism, intelligence, spirituality, and administration is one we rarely observe. Some of it is attributable to Edwards' genius, some to the simpler rhythms of his age. No longer is it possible to embody the same breadth of learning and achievement in a single person. It is possible, and Edwards would say commendable, to preach with learning and think with praying. A result of the separation of the church from the academy is a view that "spirituality" is inimical to intellectual truth, let alone practical utility. Edwards would want to encourage churches to think and universities to pray.

Edwards would challenge the contemporary church in a number of other diverse ways. But a list of what he would say if he walked into a church today only begins to suggest how relevant Edwards is to our age. Accolades cluster around Edwards like bees around a honey pot. "Greatest American theologian" is a common phrase used to praise him. Sometimes you even hear "greatest American philosopher." Frequently he is viewed as in some sense the "founder of modern evangelicalism." What makes the Edwards honey sweet, though, is that he formulated an effective response to the Enlightenment. Since Edwards, the basic shape of Western society has been framed by the Enlightenment. The Enlightenment gave birth to modern empirical science. It ushered in the formal separation of church and state. It unleashed the modern critical questions that have barraged the Bible and religious faith ever since. All this was bequeathed by the Enlightenment – the essence of which Edwards reformed. Today the Enlightenment agenda is again being considered. Our society is questioning its roots and is opting steadily for a different agenda. In this context Christians have an opportunity to formulate a new response to the Enlightenment that is distinctly Christian, with Edwards' help.

DEAD, YET SPEAKING

To find acutely relevant today a person who has been dead some three hundred years is initially surprising. C. S. Lewis reflected upon the phenomenon when he said we should read two old books for every one new book. Lewis's point was that when we read older works we have the opportunity to notice the cultural blind spots that beset our age. Similarly, the question of what Jonathan Edwards would say to contemporary life and ministry is not merely of arcane interest; it is of vital importance to the health of the modern church. With that question in mind, we turn now to Edwards. Let me introduce him as he was introduced after his first published lecture. Edwards had been invited to address a local association of Christian ministers. Impressed by his sermon, they quickly sent it to the printers. That address was called "God Glorified in Man's Dependence":

It was with no small difficulty that the author's youth and modesty were prevailed on to let him appear a preacher in our public lecture, and afterwards to give us a copy of his discourse, at the desire of the divers ministers and others who heard it. But as we quickly found him a workman that need not to be ashamed of his brethren, our satisfaction was the greater to see him pitching upon so noble a subject, and treating it with so much strength and clearness, as the judicious reader will perceive in the following composure: a subject which secures to God his great design in the work of fallen man's redemption by the Lord Jesus Christ, which is evidently so laid out, as that the glory of the whole should return to him, the blessed ordainer, purchaser, and applier; a subject which enters deep into practical religion; without the belief of which, that must soon die in the hearts and lives of men . . . And as we cannot but wish and pray that the college in the neighbouring colony (as well as our own) may be a fruitful mother of many such sons as the author, by the blessing of Heaven on the care of their present worthy rector; so we heartily rejoice in the special favor of Providence in bestowing such a rich gift on the happy church of Northampton, which has for so many lustres of years flourished under the influence of such pious doctrines, taught them in the excellent ministry of their late venerable pastor, whose gift and spirit, we hope, will long live and shine in this his grandson, to the end that they may abound yet more in all the lovely fruits of evangelical humility and thankfulness, to the glory of God.

To his blessing we commit them all, with this discourse, and everyone that reads it; and are Your servants in the gospel,

W. Cooper T. Prince
Boston, August 17, 1731.
(E. Hickman [ed.], *The Works of Jonathan Edwards* [Banner of Truth, 1988], vol. 2, p. 2)

2.

REVIVAL IS BIBLICAL

I was 14. I had recently just got going as a Christian and was part of a small and much disparaged Christian Union. The group was called the School Christian Union Meeting, or SCUM for short – an unfortunate abbreviation if ever there was one. Average attendance on a Friday evening was all of three or four pupils in a school of some five hundred or so. It was a traditional English boys' boarding school, nominally Christian in heritage and actively secular in reality. That year an evangelist secured an invitation to address the school at a series of chapel services spanning a week. During the week a total of one hundred of the five hundred pupils professed faith in Jesus Christ.

At the next meeting of the Christian Union (now changing its name to the scarcely more imaginative "Friday Meeting"), 103 people squeezed into the little room to sing, pray and listen to a basic talk from the Bible.

Historians of revival may never take note of that week, but for me it revealed God reaching modern people influenced by the Enlightenment. I know some of those converted then are now in strategic Christian ministry or exercising Christian leadership in the market-place. Undoubtedly, this early experience of mass and surprising conversions informed my expectations of what I would discover when I studied the phenomenon of revival across the world.

WHAT IS REVIVAL?

To my surprise, as I travelled to the scenes of some of the most touted modern revivals, read contemporary (as well as historical) literature about revival, and dug deep into Edwards' theology and practice of revival, I discovered that "revival" as a word carries a confusing set of possible meanings, and is commonly associated with two different and competing ideas. Strangely enough, each of these common philosophies of revival is also something of a distortion of a more fully biblical description of revival. Even more oddly, Edwards is often thought to be a proponent of one of these ideas against the other, even though actually Edwards taught neither. Adding insult to injury, revival thereby is sometimes dismissed summarily as sub-biblical, divisive or (depending on which of the competing ideas of revival you champion) emotionally manipulative. In all this the work of God in revival suffers guilt by revival association.

When many hear the word "revival" they think of an ecstatic state of near bliss. This common view is that revival is an extremely rare, humanly unattainable state of temporary overheated spirituality. Some no doubt feel this state is greatly desirable. Others (perhaps privately) rejoice that such emotional disorder is so rare. In any case, the idea is that revival appears unannounced, occasionally, spontaneously, with excitement and its own resident problems.

The alternative idea associates revival with the more mundane work of evangelistic organization. In this view, revival may be manufactured by following certain techniques or methods. This is why in the nomenclature of revivals "a revival" can become synonymous with an evangelistic campaign. As revivals follow spiritual laws much as gravity follows natural law, we may predict revivals with the certainty of knowing a lead weight dropped out of a third-floor window will fall to the ground. When we abide by the laws of revival, when we pray for so many hours or days, when we organize our meetings according to the appropriate pattern, then we can be assured that revival will be the result. We may plan a "revival week," booking it in the calendar and organizing it like a conference, with an assumption that revival will arrive on the scheduled date. Of course, to those who hold the other common view of revival, this is presumption bordering on the scandalous.

It takes little imagination to understand the pastoral challenges that can arise from these opposing views of revival. The first idea of revival so strongly emphasizes God's sovereignty that there is an inevitable tendency to passivity in evangelism. If I can do nothing to create revival, then it is understandable to wonder whether I need do anything. The second idea of revival can produce exactly the opposite challenge. If revival can be produced by a predetermined mechanism and if revival fails to arrive, spiritual disappointment, even depression, is possible, to say nothing of the pressure to produce results, which leads to spurious conversions, or those who think redemption, regeneration and revival is in their and not God's hands.

Both these ideas commonly associated with revival are caricatures. As a result, revival is sometimes opposed by its natural friends, because it has become guilty by association. No faithful pastor wishes to have an evangelistically passive congregation. Nor do biblical Christians wish to replicate a manipulative system that may look impressive but actually hurts the souls of those involved. No-one wants conflict. So as with, in *Alice in Wonderland,* Alice's frustration with Humpty Dumpty's refusal to define a word, revival language too can cause frustration, and needs to be clarified.

WHAT DID EDWARDS MEAN BY "REVIVAL"?

When Edwards spoke of revival he often talked of it as an "awakening." In Puritan terminology an awakening was a realization of spiritual need, which might under God lead to actual regeneration. Edwards employed this traditional language to refer to a process that could end in a Christian renewing his love for Christ, to pagan Native Americans becoming Christians for the first time, or to someone from a nominal Christian culture becoming truly born again. By using this broad designation he implicitly defined revival somewhat differently from the two interpretations with which we today are most familiar. An awakening could lead to renewal, conversion, mission or a key moment in the history of God's work of redemption. Edwards' thinking about revival could be summarized as follows:

> Revival encapsulates the supreme work of God invading space-time with his powerful presence. Revivals are echoes of that great revival wrought through Jesus Christ and applied through the gift of the Holy Spirit at Pentecost. There are revivals in the Old Testament that bring the people of God back to the Word of God. The New Testament church experienced, in a sense, the great archetypal revival (focused on Jesus Christ and his atoning work): they were filled with the Spirit and bursting at the seams with messy life and action. Since the New Testament, church history has many times witnessed periodical revivals. Revival is not organized by humans. But nor is revival simply an arbitrary or unusual mechanism of God for unexpected moments. Revival is the main engine of God's salvation motorcade, expressed in preparation for Jesus Christ, in Jesus Christ himself, in the gift of the Holy Spirit, in every person who has become regenerated or born again by the work of the Spirit and in every major incursion by the church into the world. Revival means nothing more or less than *salvation* applied and extraordinarily promoted.

This implicit definition of revival is discovered throughout Edwards' ministry, writings and preaching. Jonathan Edwards had personal ministry experience of several revivals. He was a leader of two great revivals and a historian of a third. The first was a local revival centered on his church in Northampton, Massachusetts. The second is known as "The Great Awakening" or "Evangelical Awakening." It spanned two continents, saw many converted, inspired much social reform as well as evangelistic outreach, and was formative for the whole modern evangelical movement. Edwards was the renowned and acclaimed theologian of this revival as well as actively at the heart of the revival movement in

New England. Edwards, as we saw in the previous chapter, was also the historian of a third "awakening," this time a revival among Native Americans led by the famous missionary David Brainerd. Edwards' edition of David Brainerd's diary records Brainerd's effective missionary work in revival or "awakening" language.

Edwards became a ministerial apologist for revival. He promoted a "concert of prayer" for the purpose of encouraging international revival. He defended the awakenings as a moderate "New Light," where "Old Lights" were the forerunners of rationalistic liberalism, and radical New Lights tended towards ecstatic extremism. He was also a pastoral model for promotion of revival and believed an "awakening" could be stimulated by fervent effectual prayer of the people of God initiated by God. Such seasons of revival were days of urgency because no-one could restart the engine of revival in their own power. Spiritual leadership was required to ensure the fires of revival would not be doused by fake emotionalism or rationalistic critics. Edwards published many books about revival, including *A Narrative of Surprising Conversions, Distinguishing Marks of a Work of God, Some Thoughts Concerning the Revival,* and finally his magnum opus on spiritual experience and revival, *A Treatise Concerning The Religious Affections.* However, the writing that contributes most to Edwards' special view of revival is a book that seems to be mainly about history. Originally a sermon series, then published as The *History of the Work of Redemption,* it had two aims. First, it was an attempt to buttress historical knowledge against the encroachments of the growing secularist-humanist philosophy of the Enlightenment. Edwards did this by describing the past as factually coinciding with the biblical narrative. Second, it was an apologetic for the enduring significance and central importance of revival to the kingdom of God. Edwards did this by depicting revival as key to salvation history. Jesus Christ was of course the atoning center of salvation, but salvation was applied and advanced by revival. Each aspect of New Testament supernaturalism was analyzed under the heading of revival: salvation history leading up to Christ, Christ's work itself, the gift of the Holy Spirit at Pentecost, regeneration, the apostolic missions, and every major growth and success of the church. Edwards wrote of revival as the sovereign work of God. Humans cannot "make" revival happen any more than they can make a person born again, or make God send Jesus, or make the Holy Spirit appear at Pentecost. In Edwards' writings revival is broader and more significant than mere ecclesiastic excitement – revival is the most effective way God grows his kingdom.

Furthermore, Edwards was a famous preacher of revival. Probably the best way to get a sense of what Edwards meant by revival is to hear one of his revival sermons. The most famous of these is called *Sinners in the Hands of an Angry God.* Despite its fearful title, and the frightening language that permeates much of the sermon, the thrust of the message is more gracious than a cursory reading would initially reveal. In essence, Edwards tells his hearers that nothing keeps them out of hell other than the goodness and mercy of God. He is preaching to a congregation (not his own) who in the midst of great revival have remained hardened to the advances of the kingdom. He urges his stony-hearted audience to make the most of the time:

> And now you have an extraordinary opportunity, a day wherein
> Christ has thrown the door of mercy wide open, and stands in
> calling, and crying with a loud voice to poor sinners; a day wherein
> many are flocking to him, and pressing into the kingdom of God.
> Many are daily coming from the east, west, north, and south; many
> that were very lately in the same miserable condition that you are in,
> are now in a happy state, with their hearts filled with love to him who
> has loved them, and washed them from their sins in his own blood,
> and rejoicing in the hope of the glory of God. How awful it is to be
> left behind at such a day! To see so many others feasting while you
> are pining and perishing! To see so many rejoicing and singing for
> joy of heart, while you have cause to mourn for sorrow of heart, and
> howl for vexation of spirit! How can you rest one moment in such a
> condition? Are not your souls as precious as the souls of people at
> Suffield, where they are flocking from day to day to Christ?
> (E. Hickman [ed.], *The Works of Jonathan Edwards* [Banner of Truth,
> 1988], vol. 2, p. 11)

Reading Edwards' sermons, I am constantly struck by a sense of how much of our preaching today is play-preaching. His sermons seem far more closely in line with the preaching of John the Baptist or the prophets of the Old Testament. There is joyful imagery at times, in the form of parables, as Christ loved to use. There is rationality and reason to match a Paul. There is always a sense of being in earnest. These days many seem to preach in jest. Edwards' preaching could be hard to swallow for those used to sermonic catering to suit their palates. Earlier in the same sermon Edwards had proclaimed:

> It is everlasting wrath. It would be dreadful to suffer this fierceness and wrath of Almighty God one moment; but you must suffer it to all eternity. There will be no end to this exquisite horrible misery. When you look forward, you shall see a long forever, boundless duration before you, which will swallow up your thoughts, and amaze your soul; and you will absolutely despair of ever having any deliverance, any end, any mitigation, any rest at all. You will know certainly that you must wear out long ages, millions of millions of ages, in wrestling and conflicting with this almighty merciless vengeance; and then when you have so done, when so many ages have actually been spent by you in this manner, you will know that all is but a point to what remains. So that your punishment will indeed be infinite. Oh who can express what the state of a soul in such circumstances is? All that we can possibly say about it, gives but a very feeble, faint representation of it; it is inexpressible and inconceivable: for 'who knows the power of God's anger?' (E. Hickman [ed.], *The Works of Jonathan Edwards* [Banner of Truth, 1988], vol. 2, p. 11)

Such sermons were not meant to please: they were intended to cure. Edwards did not only preach about hell. He certainly believed in hell and sought to warn against the "wrath to come," but it was not the only note on his rhetorical keyboard. He preached about heaven too. He also preached about love, one famous series of sermons being called *Charity and its Fruits*. In fact, Edwards is remarkable for the breadth of subjects he addressed. When people associate hellfire preaching with Edwards, it is only because it is rare to preach in such a way today. So when Edwards does mention hell, it sticks in our memory. We have heard sermons on how we should love one another, and about the truth of the Bible. But we have not heard many (or even any?) sermons about the fearful reality of hell. We may not have heard many sermons about the wonderful reality of heaven either!

Throughout his ministry, then, Jonathan Edwards understood "revival" to be a broader term than simply a momentary increased excitement. Revival included regeneration, the big salvation-historical themes of the birth and death of Jesus Christ, Pentecost and the expansion of the church. Was Edwards correct? Was he right to believe that "revivals" are central to God's salvation plan? Or should we define revivals more narrowly? The Bible seems to agree with Edwards that the idea of "revival" should be broader than the common designation of revivals or revivalism today. There are biblical reasons for resisting a restriction of the definition of a revival to a more rare and occasional moment of excitement, for insisting that revival is the sovereign work of God, and for allowing revival to be defined as a God-initiated center of the advance of his kingdom.

WHAT DOES THE BIBLE TEACH ABOUT REVIVAL?

To begin with, the Bible rarely seems to use the term *revive*. This is especially apparent in modern translations of the Bible. The New International Version (NIV) uses a variety of terms for "revive," found in the Authorized Version (AV). Ezra 9:8 reads, "give us a little reviving in our bondage" in the AV, whereas in the NIV it is "a little relief in our bondage." As the Ezra-Nehemiah catalogue of God bringing his people back from exile to rebuild the walls of Jerusalem is a classic "revival" text, even this minor linguistic change has a major influence on how revival is perceived in the general Christian world. The verbal blurring of specific revival references is not uniform, though. The AV translates Psalm 85:6 "Wilt thou not revive us again," and the NIV also has "Will you not revive us again." Later in Psalms the inconsistency of translation appears again. Psalm 138:7 is "thou wilt revive me" in the AV, but "you preserve my life" in the NIV. It should be noted that on each of these occasions the original Hebrew is the same.

When we come to the Greek New Testament, we have our first clue as to what is going on. In Romans 7 Paul describes how the Law promoted sin by giving the sinful nature a specific command to disobey. In 7:9 he says, in the AV, "when the commandment came, sin revived." Given our loaded understanding of revival today, it is understandable why the NIV instead translates this as "when the commandment came, sin sprang to life." This desire to avoid the theologically tricky word "revival" is especially obvious in the translations of Romans 14:9. There, Paul applies Jesus' death and resurrection to a Christian's need to die to his or her preferences in the Christian community. The AV says, "Christ both died, and rose, and revived." That use would never do in a day when "revival" largely carries a subjective meaning. So instead the NIV puts it "Christ died and returned to life."

The point is not that the Authorized Version is right and the New International Version wrong. By comparing an older and a newer translation of the Bible it becomes clear that the issue is not the word *revive* at all. At stake is not verbal definition (or translation) but the message of Christian supernaturalism. This idea of God entering the world, of God being "present" with his people, of God giving new life, is found so commonly in the Bible that its importance can scarcely be overstated. We could say the whole Bible is about this. The Old Testament history of Abraham and Moses, of the conquest of Canaan, of the return from exile, are all descriptions of God's supernatural action. The prophets frequently call people back to trust God and rely upon his initiative and commands. The psalms often ask God to act on behalf of his people for their salvation. The New Testament Gospels, the book of Acts, the letters to the churches, the Pastoral Epistles, even the book of Revelation, are documents witnessing to and dealing with 'revival' in this broad sense of Christian supernaturalism. The idea, though, is certainly not always connected verbally to "revival."

Psalm 80, for example, has the repeated refrain

Restore us, O God;
   make your face shine upon us,
   that we may be saved.

This verse is repeated three times in a psalm of no more than nineteen verses. It twice occupies a poetic bridging position between stanzas developing the same idea of restoration. It is the final word of the psalm as the last verse. The same concept is found elsewhere in the psalm:

Return to us, O God Almighty!
   Look down from heaven and see!
(verse 14)

Awaken your might;
   come and save us.
(verse 2)

Nowhere in this psalm does the New International Version or the Authorized Version translate "revive." Nonetheless, the psalm is an appeal for God's holy presence and his saving power. The model is the supernatural intervention that God's Old Testament people had experienced previously at the exodus:

You brought a vine out of Egypt;
   you drove out the nations and planted it.
You cleared the ground for it,
   and it took root and filled the land.
The mountains were covered with its shade,
   the mighty cedars with its branches.
It sent out its boughs to the Sea,
   its shoots as far as the River.
(verses 8–11)

The psalm asks God to intervene like that. It is not a prayer for renewed excitement or for an evangelistic mission, but is a deep recognition of the need for divine action.

Once we begin to interpret the biblical material by the spirit and not the letter, by its intention and not merely its form, we find the *idea* of revival is widespread. Surely the ministry of John the Baptist is God reviving his work of salvation? "People went out to him from Jerusalem and all Judea and the whole region of the Jordan. Confessing their sins, they were baptized by him in the Jordan River" (Matthew 3:5–6). John the Baptist is more than just a revival: he is the transitional figure between the Old Testament prophets and the arrival of the Messiah. Jesus tells us he was the greatest of the prophets because he not only predicted the Christ but set eyes upon Jesus himself. Yes, John the Baptist is *more* than a revival figure, but surely his ministry is not *less* than a revival?

Or consider the influence and activities associated with Pentecost. Surely this too is a revival:

> All of them were filled with the Holy Spirit and began to speak in
> other tongues as the Spirit enabled them . . . Peter stood up with
> the Eleven, raised his voice and addressed the crowd . . . When
> the people heard this, they were cut to the heart . . . Those who
> accepted his message were baptized, and about three thousand were
> added to their number that day. (Acts 2:4, 14, 37, 41)

Again, we should not think that Pentecost was only or merely a typical revival, as this occurrence had some unique facets. What is unique about Pentecost and what is typical of all revivals is controversial in Christian circles. Is speaking in tongues a unique aspect of Pentecost, indicating the new work of the Spirit going to all nations? Or is it typical of the work of the Spirit in the new era of Pentecost that the unique Pentecost inaugurated? But that there is something typical as well as unique about Pentecost, all agree. It ushers in a new time of the Holy Spirit: Peter tells us as much. He preaches repentance as a result. Many are baptized and converted. Surely these elements of Pentecost are typical revival features?

The missionary work of the apostle Paul had a similar dual function. Yes, Paul was unique. He was an apostle and his missionary work was pioneering in some ways that no subsequent missionary work could be. But Paul's ministry was also typical of revivals:

our gospel came to you not simply with words, but also with power,
with the Holy Spirit and with deep conviction . . . you welcomed the
message with the joy given by the Holy Spirit. And so you became
a model to all the believers in Macedonia and Achaia. The Lord's
message rang out from you not only in Macedonia and Achaia – your
faith in God has become known everywhere. (1 Thessalonians 1:5–8)

Paul enthuses with understandable hyperbole (their faith had become
known "everywhere") because their awakening or revival or supernatural
conversion and the planting of their church was a true model to other
believers. Surely the Corinthian church as well as the Thessalonian, and
the other churches of the New Testament age, while unique in being the
first recipients of the gospel of Jesus, nonetheless also function as models
to us of what it is like for missionary work to advance or for churches to
be renewed?

Interpreting the material by the spirit of the sense of the passages and
not the letter of verbal definition, by context and principle, not word
similarities in dictionaries of terms used in the New Testament, we find
that the *idea* of revival is centrally important to New Testament Christianity. In fact, we can go further. Jesus himself is revival. Of course Jesus
is unique. His is "the glory of the One and Only, who came from the
Father, full of grace and truth" (John 1:14). But Jesus is also a template
for us of what Christian living, ministry and teaching should be like. If
he is only unique and not also a model, we are stranded upon the shores
of dissimilarity: as C. S. Lewis once remarked, we are, in some sense, to
become "little Jesuses." Jesus' ministry is a revival. It is a God-initiated
supernatural invasion from heaven. It is *the* revival, we should say, of
which all others are shadows (in the Old Testament) or echoes (in the
New Testament age).

Undoubtedly there are reasons why the Bible does not mechanistically
employ exactly the same term every time it talks about revival. Actually I
am hard pressed to think of any significant theological concept the Bible
always describes by using the same word. Perhaps especially with revival
it is necessary to safeguard the concept against our human tendency to
want to control God. The natural progress of the spirit is from rebellion

to religious moral reformation; only when we see God, or accept God, as the necessary source of our moral regeneration can any divine progress, real reformation (or revival, awakening, enlightening), happen.

The history of revival shows a constant slide towards "revivalism," the lamentable desire to put God in a box and get him to do what we want by means of certain religious techniques. But, biblically speaking, even the term "revival" is more slippery than that. God will not be controlled or magically conjured up. Revival is a statement of God's initiative. It is not simply evangelistic decisions, nor merely more-determined and disciplined Christians: it is the outpouring of the Spirit in might and power, such that we are caught up to the fullness of New Testament Christianity.

WHAT IS WRONG WITH OUR IDEAS ABOUT REVIVAL?

In the contemporary church, however, the practice of revival can be less ideal. It can be manipulative. It can engender passivism among Christians "watching and praying" (but not also working and preaching) or sometimes merely watching. I have been to revival meetings where the enthusiastic contributors have literally attempted to waft (I can think of no better word) the Holy Spirit from one part of the room to another by physically waving their hands, as if the wind of the Spirit could be blown around with an electric fan. I have also watched how "revivalism," or the idea of bringing a revival to town, like a campaign event, has created stomach-churning temporary religious carnivals, circus-like in their presentation as well as their seemingly poor long-term influence. It is hard to feel God is honored when a program for a revival, for instance, also gives away free coupons for cheeseburgers!

Revival is criticized mainly because of this guilt by association. If you pick up a dictionary and look up the word "revival," it will most likely be defined in terms of a momentary increased and well-organized carnival of religious excitement. You can hear the cynicism breathe through such definitions. Understandably enough, many wish to distance themselves from revival terminology. Some also say that "large-meeting evangelism" has had its day, that such techniques are now passé. Edwards' approach to revival is so different that we might almost wish we could invent a new term to describe it. Perhaps the old Puritan phrase "awakening" has more merit. Describing revivals as awakenings might help distinguish means (how we do evangelism) from message (what we preach) and Master (who regenerates and revives). Even though we do not have the luxury of rewriting all the dictionaries in the world, we can at least be clear here as to what we mean by the word. Revival is not random, not manipulative, not tied to a particular system or certain ecclesiastical machine. It is God's initiative, his action, his intervention, his applying salvation to the church and the world.

Much of the contemporary criticism of revival is well founded. Revivalism can be manipulative and shallow, its techniques unthinkingly aping modernistic attitudes of industrialism and individualism, and woefully inadequate to anticipate the changing culture in which we live. Revivals can also be excuses for delay, inaction and remaining passive in the face of the challenges the church is called to address. All these and other criticisms targeted towards revivals are at least to some degree cogent. Edwards would have agreed: for him, true revival was less mechanical and more magisterial, less passive and more powerful and Christ-like.

PUTTING IT INTO PRACTICE

How could Edwards' principle of revival be put into practice today? A practical strategy for revival may appear a contradiction, similar to trying to arrange a natural disaster or for lightning to strike. There are reasons why these things are called "acts of God." For Edwards, though, while revival could not arbitrarily be generated by humans, there were "means" that could be employed to make it more likely for revival to occur. It is possible and advisable to prepare for acts of God even if we cannot make God act. Another analogy is conversion. While we cannot make ourselves born again, this gives us no excuse to avoid hearing biblical preaching, praying to Jesus to save us or the like. Salvation is a gift of grace, but it still needs to be received by faith. It is true that this faith is also the work of God, but that does not mean we should avoid exercising it if we find we can. Revival is similarly an act of God with, according to Edwards, divinely revealed biblical means. If Edwards is correct, we may have found one way to have that much-desired profound impact on our postmodern society, a culture of post-Christian religious sophisticates for whom not only is the gospel not "good news"; it is no longer "news" at all. Revival Edwards-style may be just the awakening we need. Edwards' theology of revival cannot be dumbed down to a few practical applications. Risking shocking simplification, therefore, the following suggestions towards a strategic practice of revival today may prove useful.

Revive preaching

Edwards' preaching was never revivalistic in the sense of being emo-tionally manipulative. Dr. Martyn Lloyd-Jones memorably described preaching as "logic on fire," and Edwards' sermons came close to that ideal. There was an emotional or convicting thrust to the sermon. There was also a logical or exegetical foundation. This kind of preaching was central to Edwards' practice of revival. If we want revival, we need to learn to preach. We need to revive preaching to have revival.

The failure of the Enlightenment project has influenced the church in numerous ways, but nowhere more acutely than in its preaching. Because we are suspicious of rationalism or objectivity or claims to ultimate truth, the form of preaching (which implies truth to be delivered) is suspect. Preaching therefore becomes more sentimental. Preachers tell stories because – as we all know – Jesus told stories, for-getting that Jesus' stories were all retellings of the great story of God's redemption plan. Preachers should not tell stories; they should tell the story. But it is this big story, or metanarrative, that is subverted by our cultural taste, and consequently rarely delivered from our pulpits.

Preaching becomes more suggestive, more dialogical, aping the interactive style of modern lecturing sophists, the self-help gurus or the stand-up comedians.

Reviving preaching today would be a sign that God is reviving his church. A greater commitment to careful explanation of the text would be married with a relevant and emotionally engaged application. There would be no overreaction against the sentimentalism of our culture to the anachronistic escapism of dusty rationalism. There would be logic indeed; there would also be fire. It would not be preaching in eighteenth-century terminology, nor preaching the "old way." Instead it would be preaching the old message in a new way appropriately tailored to suit the ancient message.

Excellent preachers tend to be exemplary, and Edwards is no exception. He exemplifies a care with the text. There is a straightforward transparency to his proclamation that mimics Paul's commitment to avoid underhand techniques (2 Corinthians 4:2). Edwards also models rigorous personal Bible study. Too many of our contemporary preachers seem to spend more time on the phone than in the Bible. If new light is to break into our world, it will be from sparks flying from the anvil of disciplined study of the Scriptures. Edwards' preaching was neither boring nor irrelevant nor superficial. It was *electric*. It was straightforward explanatory teaching of Bible passages, but it was also evangelistic. There was indeed something special about Edwards' preaching, parallel to his unique personality and the way God chose to use him. But Edwards' principle of emphasizing the message of the Bible and proclaiming it may be generalized to lesser mortals and different times.

Today there is a great hunger for the Word of God. Sheep need feeding, and our churches languish for lack of teaching. Those who walk in darkness need enlightening, and our society stumbles for lack of prophetic biblical vision. Neither feeding nor enlightening implies speaking in the language of Zion or boring all to distraction, however. It does mean worship services with enough time for the message of the Bible, open Bibles and expectant hearts when listening to preaching, and evangelism and mission strategically centered upon a proclamation of the Bible. The Scriptures say that the sword of the Spirit is the word of God (Ephesians 6:17). My Sunday-school teacher made us recite that verse every Sunday morning. We put our Bibles under our arms ("sheathed our swords"). We then took them out and hastened in the quickest possible fashion to find the Bible verse he had given us. While it may be childish to replicate that game in adult church, this kind of activity would at least remind us of the spiritual power of the Bible. Dare any call childish a commitment to the word that is the power of salvation to those who believe (Romans 1:16)? Put away the projector and instead take out the Bible. The preached word need not be dry, boring or unattractive. It is fire, life, a sword.

Revive the church

Edwards' practice of revival centered upon the local church. In his day familiar "parachurch" organizations such as the Universities and Colleges Christian Fellowship did not exist. No want of entrepreneurial spirit inhibited the formation of such societies, but there was a theological commitment to the church, for Edwards had a high view of the church. This should not be confused with a high-church theology. He recognized that, in the well-worn statement of our day, "The church was God's Plan A and he didn't have a Plan B." People can be turned off to "the church," perhaps through poor personal experience of local communities. Even when someone complains about the church, though, they often inadvertently establish its significance. Anger at God at some point will involve frustration with the church, for it is the church that carries Christ's name and the church that represents him in the modern world. Genuine revival, then, will not merely bring more effective preachers and evangelists. The church too needs to be revived, because communities of salt and light are necessary for such preaching to be realistically and practically modeled. Without free samples of Christ the message of Christ is hard to swallow.

Jesus said the gates of hell would not prevail against his church. So he obviously knew the gates of hell would try. The church has borne the brunt of much of the devilish attack down through the ages, and the church must be renewed for us to bring revival to our world, community, village, society or neighborhood. As such, our best thinkers and workers need to work hard together at getting the church more in line with God's truth and more effective at proclaiming Christ. A powerful evangelistic strategy in postmodern times must have this sense of community to it. Individualistic as many today are, we also long for community, for a sense of belonging, of being a part of something together. The church is where we are meant to find that. This means that church planting and church revitalization are the key mechanisms for evangelistic advance today.

What does all this have to do with "revival"? Why discuss preaching and the church? Is not revival something different altogether? Are not preaching and the church too mundane, too lacking in mystical or experiential elements to be associated with that category of revival? These questions come once more from associating "revival" with the later developments of the nineteenth century, not Edwards' eighteenth century, with a more sentimental and more mechanical approach. Our view of revival has been shaped by our experiences of "revivalism" (the carnival that came to town), or by some personal encounter with the idea. But preaching God's Word in its widest sense, and the establishment of faithful communities of gospel witness in the local church, are indeed the ways God brings revival to us. We should focus upon them, seeking first the kingdom of God and his righteousness, and understand that God by these means may bring revival and, we pray, extend his kingdom.

That great Old Testament revival, the return of the people from exile under the leadership of Ezra and Nehemiah, was characterized by twin emphases. Although the Ezra-Nehemiah revival involved confession of sin and a desire for holiness, the two means that promoted the revival were the rebuilding of the temple and the proclamation of the Law. Ezra praised God that "He has granted us new life [AV, "a reviving"] to rebuild the house of our God and repair its ruins" (Ezra 9:9). In addition to this rebuilding there was also the careful explanation of the Word of God:

"They read from the Book of the Law of God, making it clear and giving the meaning so that the people could understand what was being read" (Nehemiah 8:8). We need to focus on both these means of revival. Many of our churches, not the buildings but the people, are in a state of disrepair, of unbiblical compromise and sin, of lazy inattention and being stuck in the past. We need to rebuild our communities. We also need to explain the Bible, for there is a basic ignorance of what the Bible says and actually means. How can they believe if they do not know what we are asking them to believe (Romans 10:14)?

Spiritual revival

Edwards did emphasize the church and the Bible, but he also described other means of promoting revival. He believed in the importance of personal testimony as an encouragement to others to seek God. As already mentioned, he was a pioneer in developing a '"concert of prayer," an international commitment to pray together for revival. Furthermore, "the Word" and "the church" were never for Edwards merely logical or institutional: he viewed them as dynamic entities empowered by the living presence of the Holy Spirit. The great modern controversy about the work of the Spirit is not evoked by Edwards, because he lived long before us. It is true there were similar discussions in Edwards' day concerning ecstatic manifestations, and, as we have seen, he taught that the supernatural gifts of the Spirit could not be expected to return. Nonetheless, several centuries later we still get the distinct impression of spiritual vitality, that subjective and indefinable quality of spiritual power, of the Holy Spirit's personal anointing, of God's energizing presence and the Heavenly Father's blessing.

If spiritual revival is ecclesiastically controversial today, it is also manifestly necessary. The levels of holiness, of the fear of the Lord, of simple spiritual power, are at a low ebb in the West. Previous to the awakenings, Edwards describes a similar "low state into which the visible church of God has lately been sunk" (E. Hickman [ed.], *The Works of Jonathan Edwards* [Banner of Truth], 1988, vol. 2, p. 272). He concludes that, despite the unusual manifestations, the controversial issues that have become stumbling blocks for some, the movement is, "undoubtedly, in the general, from the Spirit of God" (ibid., p. 269). He urges his readers "by no means to oppose, or do any thing in the least to clog or hinder, the work; but, on the contrary, do our utmost to promote it" (ibid., p. 272). Addressing the doubters directly, he tells them it is "better to speak against God the Father, or the Son, than to speak against the Holy Spirit in his gracious operations on the hearts of men." And "I would beg of them to take heed that they be not guilty of the unpardonable sin" (ibid., p. 273) by speaking against the Holy Spirit. So while Edwards' much-attributed aphorism "the task of every generation is to discover in which way the Sovereign Redeemer is moving and then to move in that direction" (ibid.) was never recorded as uttered by him, it still expresses something Edwards held dear.

We must not forget that while Edwards was partly a traditionalist he was also an innovator. The whole concept of a "Great Awakening" was controversial in Edwards' time precisely because it seemed novel (preaching in the fields) and dangerous (disorderly excitements). We too need to learn the necessity of following the work of the Holy Spirit. Edwards' approach to revival was principally supernaturalist. As a society we have become more visual and less verbal, more musical and less prosaic, more captivated by experience and encounter than by preaching and the church. Hard as it may be to believe now, in times gone by there was a danger some would go to listen to preachers purely for entertainment value. We cannot nor should we aim to return to those days. Edwards' philosophy of revival does not amount to an anachronistic call to the past: his principled reliance upon divine initiative engenders a forward movement. Edwards expected to encounter God, not just empowerment from God. He wanted not merely a sip at the fountain of life, but a drink that would become wells of living water from within. No methodology itself suffices, but only the work of the Spirit of God.

A hunger for spiritual revival must increasingly characterize our practice of prayer, preaching, evangelism, church business meetings, devotional lives, families and all else – if the Western church is to revive.

We must follow where God goes. He will surprise and change us. He would lead us forward, not just in the old ways, but in new ways too.

Edwards' theology of revival has three practical and strategic implications. First, it encourages us to emphasize preaching. Second, it calls us to focus upon the basics of building local churches. Third, it points us forward through the power of the Holy Spirit.

Revival as an unbiblical and manipulative belief in the capability of human agency to generate spiritual change must be eschewed. Revival meaning a passive and stagnant excuse for doing nothing because God has not brought revival needs to be exposed for what it is: an attitude foreign to the vigorous missionary effort and evangelism modeled by the apostle Paul. Revival as a principled reliance upon and expectation of divine initiative for the advance of the kingdom through God-given means is what we should embrace.

3.

TRUE EXPERIENCE OF GOD
IS HEART EXPERIENCE

Several times now I have come across people in a pastoral context whose perception of their experience of God has become dangerously skewed. Some have even thought he was telling them not to eat. Granted, the Bible does encourage us to fast occasionally. Nonetheless, when the supposed command from God not to eat is taken to a dangerous medical extreme, it is not only legitimate to wonder whether the spiritual experience is genuine, but it is imperative to seek professional help. I have come across other even weirder messages purportedly received from God. The psychological difference between people who think God is telling them to cut their wrists and those who think they are Napoleon is not as great as we might wish.

Suffice it to say that Christian leaders do not always greet enthusiastically the claim "God is speaking to me." Of course, people who feel they have a word from God do not necessarily need psychiatric care. Christians believe in a speaking God who has spoken and still speaks today. It is the idols that are dumb. But while it may be relatively easy to discern a mental imbalance camouflaged in religious language, other more mundane and subtle confusion can arise from high claims to spiritual experience. If someone says, "I feel the Spirit is leading us," it could mean they are especially sensitive to God's direction. It could also really mean they want something and are using religious jargon, perhaps unconsciously, to manipulate the situation to their own ends. Claims of spiritual experience can be profound, profoundly self-deceived or even profane, not to mention positively devilish, for Satan masks himself as an "angel of light" (2 Corinthians 11:14). How do you discern? Examples of this kind of difficulty could be multiplied. The central issue is how to discern the reliability of personal spiritual experience of God. Christianity claims, if it claims anything at all, that those who are Christians have a personal relationship with God.

But what does this mean? Does this mean God tells me which kind of lunch to eat? And if not, why not? Surely that would be useful information – might help me diet – and would certainly be at least a form of personal relationship? If God does not or cannot be frequently expected to speak in this kind of direct manner, what does it mean to have a personal relationship with him?

Are we talking about feelings? In what sense are those feelings different from sentimental emotions that may be evoked in others at the sight of a sunset or a beautiful building, or that seem in plentiful supply around a candlelit dinner? If these are the self-same emotions evoked by these alternative environments, should we be skeptical of the church's use of, for instance, music, or architecture, or the language of "relationship" as an attempt to produce emotions that make objective sense in those settings, but which are only superficially connected with religion? I take it that most of the readers of this chapter believe that in some sense we are expected to have a personal relationship with God, and for reasons too many to enumerate here. But if we are expected to have this connection with God, why at times do we feel like we do not? Are we fooling ourselves when at other times we feel like we do?

Perhaps "feelings" of personal relationship with God are not so definitive. There are many psalms in the Bible in which the author clearly confesses his lack of a sense of feeling close to God. Psalm 43:5, for example, says:

Why are you downcast, O my soul?
    Why so disturbed within me?
Put your hope in God,
    for I will yet praise him,
    my Savior and my God.

This suggests a strong personal relationship with God may exist not only without but despite feelings of intimacy. Why, then, should I expect profound experience of God to be marked by feeling close to God? Should I consider a personal relationship with God as like being in a permanent state of the early stages of a love affair? Is a personal relationship with God more like a 40-year-old marriage, in which the feelings are still there, but the flames burn lower? Or is a personal relationship with God similar to a friendship with your bank manager? There are limits to the closeness of the friendship, but you are glad you have such an important relationship with such a powerful person in your life – especially if you should need a loan. Is that what a friendship with God is like? Is he your ultimate boss, who remains relationally your boss but with whom you are glad you are sort of on the "inside track"?

These and other questions about spiritual experience all come back to the same point: the need to discern true from false spiritual experience. Ineptitude in this area has allowed crass manipulation to flourish in many a local church, hostage to the "God told me" trump card. It has also led to confusion, uncertainty and a fear of spiritual experience like a fear of the unknown. Not a million miles away, heresies in the form of Mormonism, Christian Science and Jehovah's Witnesses have flourished in the experiential vacuum. Then there are the hosts of individual Christians who deny clear teaching in Scripture, because what the Bible says goes against what they feel – and, after all, they have a personal relationship with God.

THE SIGNIFICANCE OF EDWARDS' APPROACH

Edwards had two theological mechanisms for discernment. He had a "sense" of true experience (which we will consider in this chapter) and "signs" of true experience (which we will consider in the next). They belong together and inform one another as roots lead to fruits. The "sense" of true experience is especially important because it gets to the "epistemological" cause of all this confusion about experiencing God. Epistemology is the study of how we know things. When we say we have a personal relationship with God we are making an extraordinary epistemological claim, because we are saying we know God personally ("epistemology" is the theory of knowledge). Edwards' "sense" of true experience addresses the problem of how we can know we are experiencing God.

This problem has gained great historical momentum. Western society is reeling from an earthquake in our epistemological foundations that took place several centuries ago. The story is complex, but without too much distortion we may summarize it like this. Medieval society had an epistemology of authority. Modern society has an epistemology of science. "Postmodern" or "emerging" culture has an epistemology of relativism. The shift from medieval to modern ways of thinking occurred from the sixteenth-century Reformation to the eighteenth-century Enlightenment. After the Reformation regained a confidence in Scripture (the "Book of God"), the Enlightenment discovered a confidence in science and reason (the "Book of Nature").

The change from modern to postmodern attitudes is still under way. It began with such seminal thinkers as Friedrich Nietzsche, sometimes called the "grandfather of postmodernism." More recently, Michel Foucault and Jacques Derrida led the way towards a radical undermining of both Reformation and Enlightenment confidence in knowledge. But postmodernism is not really intellectual: it is a gut feeling of distrust of authoritative pronouncements and an assumption that society functions best by tolerance: to be tolerant of people of different faiths and cultures one must accept that there is no "truth" about such matters.

There are lots of ironies in the story that may even be apparent from this brief synopsis. Modern attitudes to life were generated within religious frameworks, but became radically critical of religion. Postmodern relativism frowns on all truth claims, yet is itself an absolute truth claim! But the historical narrative does more than contextualize

Edwards' contribution within a sea of epistemological confusion. It also indicates the precise significance of his view of "spiritual epistemology." Edwards lived at the start of the Enlightenment. Yet he stood apart from it. He responded to the Enlightenment attitude to God and the possibility of spiritual experience. Edwards' spiritual epistemology was ruggedly biblical, emotionally appealing and intellectually credible. As we are heirs to the Enlightenment's epistemological fragmentation, Edwards' approach clarifies what is and what is not true experience of God in our lives today.

His was a "sense" of true experience. Edwards said the "sense of the heart" was genuine spiritual experience. It is an evocative turn of phrase, suggestive of vaguely romantic or emotional connotations. Edwards, though, was drawing upon his Christian theology to respond to the Enlightenment. Experience of God was a "sense" in touch with the sensibility of contemporary empirical science. Spiritual experience was "heart" experience in counterbalance to the Enlightenment emphasis on the rational "head," which Edwards wanted to both affirm and challenge. Each of these emphases emerged from a God-centered view of spiritual experience. His understanding of spiritual experience was not self-orientated but was God-focused. His theology of salvation meant that personal relationship with God could not be based on how we felt; instead, it had to rely upon the objective work of Christ on the cross, revealed to us by the Spirit through the Bible. This Reformation theology and evangelical passion are the backbone of Edwards' writings on personal experience, and apply acutely in a day when we tend to have a more self-orientated view of spiritual experience. It is this "sense of the heart" that Edwards expresses in his regular preaching, published sermons, books and personal journals.

WHAT EDWARDS SAYS ABOUT THE SENSE OF THE HEART

Edwards used "sense" terminology frequently in his sermons. Experience of God is a "sight" of God. Preaching on Hebrews 11:27, "[Moses] saw him who is invisible," Edwards taught about the seeing nature of Christian faith. Obviously Moses did not physically see God, yet Edwards believed he saw God with the eyes of faith. Edwards stressed the directness of Moses' personal relationship with God. In this way he was appealing to our trust in empirical data, that "seeing is believing" and that scientific conclusions are reliable. It is by faith that Moses saw God, but this "faith sight" is a real and true knowledge of the invisible God, in the same way that when we see physical objects we assume we have received reliable information.

Edwards made a similar point in his sermons on the beginning of 2 Peter. The apostle Peter says the apostles were "eyewitnesses" of Jesus' "majesty" (2 Peter 1:16), describing the transfiguration of Jesus, which Peter observed with his physical eyes. Peter underlines his eyewitness status so his readers might understand that the message of the gospel is something he has not invented. He did not "follow cleverly invented stories" but was a direct observer of Christ. When Edwards preached on these passages he connected this direct experience to the later message in the chapter about our spiritual experience of God. He said we too have the possibility of direct personal relationship with God, that we may also experience the "morning star," which "rises in your hearts" (2 Peter 1:19).

The published sermon *A Divine and Supernatural Light* not only proclaims the "sense" of true experience, but combines this with the "sense of the heart." Eighteenth-century titles were rather long. The full title of this sermon is no exception, but is worth repeating at length because it signifies what Edwards was saying about spiritual experience. The sermon is on Matthew 16:17, Jesus' commendation of Peter's confession of faith. The complete title of the sermon reads, *A Divine and Supernatural Light, Immediately Imparted to the Soul by the Spirit of God, Shown to be both a Scriptural and Rational Doctrine.*

For those confident in reason Edwards proclaims that spiritual experience is not only biblical; it is also rational. For those relying upon empirical sense data Edwards describes spiritual experience as a "light" "immediately imparted," in the same way light from the sun comes to our senses. For Edwards this "spiritual and divine light" was "A true sense of the divine excellency of the things revealed in the word of God" (E. Hickman [ed.], *The Works of Jonathan Edwards* [Banner of Truth], 1988, vol. 2, p. 14). The experience is a "sense," a sight (as he said later in the same sermon, a "seeing") of the "divine excellency." By "excellency" Edwards means what makes God objectively beautiful. It is one of Edwards' technical terms, derived from the idea that God's goodness is aesthetically beautiful and beauty is objectively excellent.

Edwards is not saying *any* experience will do. It must be an experience of the "divine excellency." Nor is he saying the experience may give us any kind of information about God. To be genuine, the experience must be of the "things revealed in the word of God," it *must* be biblical, lead to a relish of biblical truth, and not pretend to teach new information not found in the Bible. Despite this Word-driven aspect of the experience, Edwards is also careful to avoid the charge of bibliolatry. God is the immediate cause of the experience, not the Bible. And, though the experience must be biblical, it also must not be rationalistic. Certainly the "divine and supernatural light" is rational in that it stimulates and promotes reason. However, it is not reason that perceives God. Spiritual experience of God "is not a speculative thing, but depends on the sense of the heart." Or, as he said:

> Reason's work is to perceive truth and not excellency. It is not ratio-
> cination that gives men the perception of the beauty and amiable-
> ness of a countenance, though it may be many ways indirectly an
> advantage to it; yet it is no more reason that perceives it, than it
> is reason that perceives the sweetness of honey: it depends on the
> sense of the heart. (Hickman, *Works of Jonathan Edwards*, vol. 2, pp.
> 16, 17)

How surprising was Edwards! Here was a man who had, to quote Marvin the Paranoid Android from the *Hitchhiker's Guide to the Galaxy*, a brain the size of the universe, clearly arguing (rationally and scripturally) that, while reason is involved in our "personal relationship with God," it is not reason but the "sense of the heart" that perceives the experience of God.

Edwards' books also taught this "sense of the heart." In the *Religious Affections* he argued in favor of emotion as an essential component of true spiritual experience. Edwards could not conceive how someone could genuinely experience God and also remain emotionally cold:

> That religion which God requires, and will accept, does not consist in weak, dull and lifeless wouldings [desired acts or resolves of godliness rather than fulfilled ones], raising us but a little above the state of indifference: God, in his Word, greatly insists upon it, that we be in good earnest, fervent in spirit, and our hearts vigorously engaged in religion. (J. E. Smith, H. S. Stout and K. P. Minkema [eds.], *A Jonathan Edwards Reader* [Yale University Press, 1995], p. 143)

Edwards said that no-one was ever genuinely converted whose affections were not moved to passion for God. However, these "religious affections" were not simply equivalent to what we call "emotions." They were the "affections of the mind," the "inclination of the will." This was the "heart," but Edwards' view of the heart included more rational aspects than we commonly designate by the word "heart" today. Edwards was quite explicit about the importance of balance here, although we tend to run to extremes. While a few years before writing the *Religious Affections* he observed that any kind of religious affection was embraced as of God, now, he says, many have run to the other extreme where any kind of excited religious affection is viewed as necessarily not of God. Instead, because of our psychological nature, affections are actually necessary for any behavior:

> Such is man's nature, that he is very inactive, any otherwise than he is influenced by some affection, either love or hatred, desire, hope, fear or some other. These affections we see to be the springs that set men agoing, in all the affairs of life, and engage them in all their pursuits: these are the things that put men forward, and carry 'em along, in all their worldly business; and especially are men excited and animated by these, in all affairs, wherein they are earnestly engaged, and which

they pursue with vigor. (Smith, Stout and Minkema, *Jonathan Edwards Reader*, p. 145)

Humans are motivated by their hearts, therefore:

Nothing is more manifest in fact, than that the things of religion take hold of men's souls, no further than they affect them. There are multitudes that often hear the Word of God, and therein hear of those things that are infinitely great and important, and that most nearly concern them, and all that is heard seems to be wholly ineffectual upon them, and to make no alteration in their disposition of behavior; and the reason is, they are not affected with what they hear . . . I am bold to assert, that there never was any considerable change wrought in the mind or conversation of any one person, by anything of a religious nature, that ever he read, heard or saw, that had not his affections moved. (Smith, Stout and Minkema, *Jonathan Edwards Reader*, p. 145)

Edwards was careful to establish the biblical foundation for this conclusion about the centrality of affections in spiritual experience. His text in the *Religious Affections* was 1 Peter 1:8, "Whom having not seen, ye love; in whom, though now ye see *him* not, yet believing, ye rejoice with joy unspeakable and full of glory" (AV). Edwards explained how the suffering that was the experience of the recipients of this letter of 1 Peter may promote true spiritual experience. In this context, those believing in Jesus had "a supernatural principle of love to something *unseen;* they loved Jesus Christ, for they saw him spiritually . . ." (Smith, Stout and Minkema, *Jonathan Edwards Reader*, p. 140). Edwards showed that this "sense" terminology was taught clearly in the Bible. Here was Edwards' exposition of this archetypal spiritual experience:

In rejoicing with this joy, their minds are filled, as it were, with a glorious brightness, and their natures exalted and perfected: it was a most worthy, noble rejoicing . . . It was a prelibation of the joy of heaven, that raised their minds to a degree of heavenly blessedness: it filled their minds with the light of God's glory, and made 'em themselves to shine with some communication of that glory. (Smith, Stout and Minkema, *Jonathan Edwards Reader*, p. 140)

Once this exegetical foundation was laid, Edwards argued that true spiritual experience was the "sense of the heart." It is not new information about God, but an appreciation of God: spiritual understanding primarily consists in a "sense of the supreme beauty" of God. On judgment day it is this "sense" that will mark out Christian experience from non-Christian. Christians will have this sense of his beauty: "Spiritual understanding primarily consists in this sense or taste of the moral beauty of divine things; so that no knowledge can be called spiritual, any further than it arises from, and has this in it" (Smith, Stout and Minkema, *Jonathan Edwards Reader*, section 4, part 4). It is the heart that is central, "for," he would say, "who will deny that true religion consists, in a great measure, in . . . the fervent exercises of the heart?" (ibid., p. 143).

A similar description of spiritual experience was given in Edwards' book *Some Thoughts Concerning the Revival* (part 1, section 5). As a preeminent record of the ideal spiritual experience, Edwards records one of his parishioners, whom scholars later identified as none other than his wife, as:

More than once continuing for five or six hours together, without any interruption, in that clear and lively view or sense of the infinite beauty and amiableness of Christ's person, and the heavenly sweetness of his excellent and transcendent love; so that (to use the person's own expressions) the soul remained in a kind of heavenly Elysium, and did as it were swim in the rays of Christ's love, like a little mote swimming in the beams of the sun, or streams of his light that came in at a window . . . extraordinary views of divine things, and religious affections, being frequently attended with very great effects on the body, nature often sinking under the weight of divine discoveries, the strength of the body was taken away, so as to deprive of all ability to stand or speak; sometimes the hands clinched, and the flesh cold, but senses still remaining; animal nature often in a great emotion and agitation, and the soul very often, of late, so overcome with great admiration, and a kind of omnipotent joy, as to cause the person (wholly unavoidably) to leap with all the might, with joy and mighty exultation of soul . . .

We are, again, talking about the "sense of the heart."

In various unpublished papers Edwards discussed his understanding of the "sense of the heart." Some historians mistook the language of these private papers to be a "secret" Edwards at odds with the public Edwards. Rather, they are the ammunition store for the spiritual war he waged on the front lines of preaching and publishing. In these papers Edwards simply explained what he meant by the "sense of the heart" as a direct encounter with God. The new "sense" given by God is not just a "personal relationship," like a friendship, but is a whole new taste and principle fused into the soul. The "heart" is our total psychological interweaving with God, including the mind, emotions and will. Edwards felt that this use of "heart" was a biblical way of talking, because it was an accurate representation of how the ancient Hebrews thought. Most modern scholars would agree with that analysis. When the Bible says "heart," it does not mean our feelings, nor does it mean our thinking in terms of our logic; it means the sum of our person, our gut, our thinking–willing–feeling union. What I have a heart for in biblical terms is what I want, what I am, what I believe. This is of course the operation of the mind in some way, but it's not just "what I think." Nor is it just what I feel. True spiritual experience involves the whole of me. I am given a new taste for or relish of divine things. My whole soul is orientated towards God. I have a "sense of the heart" of divine beauty.

HOW DOES THIS COMPARE WITH OTHER VIEWS?

The best way to appreciate what Edwards means by the "sense of the heart" is to compare it with other descriptions of religious experience. William James' work the *Varieties of Religious Experience* is the most influential textbook in this area. Written in 1902, James' extensive analysis of religious types, along with first-hand reports of those experiencing religion, operated within a humanistic framework analyzing religious experiences by means of sociological observation and psychological assumptions. This does not mean that James was against religion. He felt there were beneficial results of religious experience, but what these were should be assessed carefully and described acutely.

James, in some ways, used similar terms to Edwards. He also talked about a "sense," though in this case a "sense of presence." He also emphasized the importance of the emotions in the religious life, though now with a tendency to downplay the rational. What Edwards held in balance, James made contradictory. There was a "variety" of religious experience. The phenomenon of religion cannot be denied, nor is it entirely negative, James felt, but it must be analyzed psychologically. There is no objective rational basis for religious experiences, even when most edifying, and certainly not in any Christian belief in the uniqueness of Christ's atoning work on the cross for salvation. In some ways William James learnt from Jonathan Edwards, but only as the husk learnt from the kernel.

Is there anything within Edwards' "sense of the heart" that can act as antidote to this secularistic explanation? James' case relies upon the creed that, in modern life, while God may exist, one can have no public confidence he does. Religious faith is a private feeling, a sentiment, an experience, but not a description of actual reality. Edwards helps here because he describes religious experience in the language of empiricism (the theory that all knowledge comes from what the senses experience). Connection with God is not simply like a sense; it is a sense. And the experience, while beyond reason, promotes reason and generates rational achievement.

William James is out of date. Nowadays, because of the ongoing shift from modernism to postmodernism, it is not possible to claim absolutely that there is insufficient reason to believe in God. That modernistic challenge to Christianity has foundered, not through the amassing of more and more evidence in favor of Christianity, but because modernism has been exposed as unable to live up to its own standards. In a justly famous article in the academic journal Nous, Christian philosopher Alvin Plantinga argues that the traditional epistemological foundation of modern epistemology is not cogent ("Is Belief in God Properly Basic?"

Nous 15 [1981], pp. 41–51). The modernist claim is that all reliable knowledge must be based on the foundation either of our senses or of what is rationally indubitable. Plantinga points out that that theory itself is neither based on our senses, nor rationally indubitable; it is, he says, in one of the best put-downs of academic history, "self-referentially incoherent."

That means we dare no longer assume God cannot be proven. Of course, the danger is that if we do not have this 'foundationalist' approach to knowledge, we will have a relativistic approach to knowledge. Again, Edwards helps here. He describes spiritual experience as a "sense," like empirical knowledge. It is also a "sense of the heart," which includes rational perceptions but also emotional intuition; it is an inclination to God's Word in the Scriptures. So it is a defined sense, a boundaried sense. Certainly Edwards cannot, nor never intended to, answer all the problems raised by contemporary secular critiques of religious experience, but his "sense of the heart" does provide some useful channels down which to promote effective answers.

What about contemporary popular views of spiritual experience? These essentially fall into two camps, more divisive and more compelling than any denominational barrier. In the *blue* corner are those who view spiritual experience with distinct suspicion. While they would, of course, acknowledge that Christians do have a "personal relationship" with God, they tend to deny if not denounce those whose expression of that personal relationship becomes too emotional, too sentimental, too enthusiastic or too controlling a grid through which other aspects of the Christian life are viewed. They emphasize the logical, not in an academic way but in a common-sense, down-to-earth fashion.

In the *red* corner are those whose view of spiritual experience is more direct, more emotional, more intuitive. Some here may even claim experiences of God that go substantially beyond scriptural revelation. Edwards would have nothing to do with that. Some, though, would merely express their "personal relationship" with God in dynamic and intuitive expressions, full-throttle on the emotions and sometimes less carefully avoiding common-sense traps.

Edwards in some ways expresses both of these alternative options and at the same time neither. His view of the essence of spiritual experience combines what we could call a "head and heart" approach to spiritual experience and our personal relationship with God. Edwards is not against emotions. He is for a balance between these emphases of the head and heart, though he describes for good reason the essence of the affections as a "sense of the heart."

This different approach to spiritual experience has all sorts of practical ramifications. Corporate worship is not merely a matter of the emotions. Nor is it merely a matter of the mind. It is a necessary engagement of both aspects of our "heart." We should not downplay or try to pour water on excited emotions in church worship – we should expect emotions and seek them. We should stir them up, not in a manipulative or anti-rational way, but in a true and appropriate response to the incalculable glory of God! Worship is not merely mental or logical. Singing songs about God is just not the same exercise as a class in systematic theology. We should sing truth, but truth should be felt, be electric, or else we have not grasped the truth. Who can genuinely say he or she has understood the glory of God, to any degree whatever, who is not moved to tears, or joy, or to fall at the feet of the risen Lord Jesus and with the elders and living creatures of Revelation cry, "Worthy, worthy, worthy is the Lamb?"

Sermons become not merely impartations of information: they must touch the emotions too. If a sermon is to engage us in the truth of the Bible, that is, if a sermon is to teach God's Word, then to teach it truly and genuinely it must promote and exemplify an appropriate and genuine emotional response to the truths it is teaching. For someone to say in dry, unemotional tones "God is love" is an incomplete message. God is love, yes, but to understand that deeply we need to feel it as well.

Let us caricature the situation. In modern church X are the "chosen frozen" and "all heat and no light" camps. How would Edwards fit into that landscape? As we delve into the practical outworking of Edwards' theology of true spiritual experience, we begin to see how important his theory is. In essence, Edwards explains what Christians have always believed from the Bible about experience of God, but have sometimes expressed less well. All of Edwards' writings are full of quotations from Scripture. This is a *biblical theology* of spiritual experience and is a far more biblical understanding of human psychology.

Edwards does not use the word *psychology* but this is what some of his teaching about spiritual experience touches upon. We tend to view humans as psychologically behavioral or psychologically programmed, or a careful interweaving of the two emphases of the classic "nature" versus "nurture" debate about human psychology. Edwards instead describes our psychology in the way it relates to our motivations, actions and response to God. So Edwards' practical utility emerges from a profound analysis of human psychology. This then affects how humans respond to religious teaching, worship, praise, testimony and all manner of religious input. Thus, many have said that perhaps the most important textbook for a pastor training for ministry to read is Edwards' *Religious Affections:* a handbook on what motivates people and what persuades them to follow truly and passionately after God.

Edwards' understanding of spiritual experience is certainly not from an ivory tower, for he records the experiences of individuals in his congregation whom he took to be exemplary of the revival in New England generally.

Not only is this approach to spiritual experience carefully biblical; it also has a fuller, more consistent, grasp of the gospel. The gospel must be taught, but it cannot simply be taught as if it were a mathematical equation or a series of intellectual propositions. It must be genuinely understood and appropriated, and for that there must be truth content to its proclamation.

Many questions rapidly emerge from Edwards' understanding of spiritual experience. Right at the forefront of these is the question about validation. If this is what spiritual experience is like, how do we test to know whether what we or someone else or an alternative new Christian movement is experiencing is *really* from God? Edwards also addressed this at length, and it is the subject of the next chapter.

4.

WE NEED TO ANALYZE NEW CHRISTIAN MOVEMENTS BY THEIR 'FRUIT'

Those nice young men in suits and ties come knocking at your door. "Elder," the badge on the lapel says, despite the cheerful youthfulness of the smile. They say they believe in the Bible. They ask you to pray about the truth of what they are presenting. They wonder if you have read the Book of Mormon. What makes you think they are wrong? After all, a lot of people believe. On a growth scale the Church of Jesus Christ of Latter-day Saints is doing quite nicely, thank you. Some (and they are not all from Utah) even think it is the fastest-growing church in the world today. I expect some Christians reject Mormonism for the simple reason that it seems so strange. Yet on that basis alone one might not be too enamored by the true gospel either. Whoever heard of God incarnate dying on a criminal cross to save the world?

If you cannot hit a barn door at point-blank range, you will not be much good when sniper skills are required. Likewise, if we are unable to see the true nature of Mormonism clearly, heaven help us when it comes to more subtle delusions. Edwards teaches us biblical discernment in an age of multiple spiritual options.

CAN YOU BE CRITICAL WITHOUT BEING JUDGMENTAL?

The very idea of "analyzing" appears odd to some. Perhaps it feels judgmental. Why should I analyze a Christian movement? Is that not coming close to doing what Jesus commanded we not do, "Judge not, that ye be not judged" (Matthew 7:1, AV)? Or perhaps it appears the wrong way to assess. Even if we consider it right to make assessments of fads and fashions within the Christian community, "analyzing" them may seem far too cerebral. Would we not get a more accurate appraisal by what a new Christian movement *feels* like? If we feel the Spirit moving, or the atmosphere to be reverential, should we not resist any effort to analyze such a movement as an attempt to put out the Spirit's fire? Who analyzes fire?

There may be another set of concerns with this analytical approach to new Christian movements. Edwards has two items on his evaluative agenda. First, he is concerned for a "sense" of true experience. We looked at that in the last chapter. This sense is a 'sense of the heart' and we can think about it as the roots of spiritual experience. Now we consider Edwards' analysis by the "fruit" of spiritual experience, with its moral result or the character it produces. The concern here may be whether this is a *sufficient* criterion. What about doctrinal questions? What does Edwards say about those?

NOT JUST DOCTRINE

Although there was a doctrinal element, Edwards never majored on doctrinal tests. Why did Edwards, such a biblical preacher, not stress sound doctrine as a test of spiritual experience? It was partly due to his historical context. Edwards lived in a predominantly Protestant and Puritan church culture. Doctrinal questions, while at times acute, were not as defining as in our day. Society in Edwards' time had a widely accepted and tightly controlled doctrinal framework. Most people accepted these ideas at least "notionally" or formally and mentally. Our context has widely diverse opinions about ideology and doctrine and we therefore rightly emphasize doctrinal standards as more definitive.

There is another reason, though, why Edwards did not focus upon the doctrinal, a reason with profound relevance to any age. The Bible does not only give doctrinal tests; it also provides other tests (Galatians 5:22–23). The Bible teaches us that just believing the right thing is not enough. James tells us that demons believe there is one God and shudder (James 2:19). Elsewhere, the Bible discusses the merely formal or inadequate faith of some of the Israelites and even some on the fringes of the early Christian community (1 Corinthians 10:1–13). The Bible clearly assumes it is possible to have the right answers but not have the right heart (Matthew 7:24–27; Luke 6:43–45).

This being the case, more discernment is needed about new Christian movements than merely asking, "Can they sign this or that doctrinal statement?" In our contemporary context people are increasingly willing to sign almost anything because they no longer believe in absolute truth and so do not feel restricted by a statement of truth. Edwards' tests help us discern whether a new Christian movement has really appropriated the truth that it acknowledges as true, whether it has accepted and internalized it, whether it believes it in a personal and real sense, or whether it just says "Well that's true," but is not changed by the truth.

Obviously, churches and Christian organizations should have their doctrinal statements, but equally clearly that is not enough. You do not have to be an aficionado of church history to realize that sound, carefully written doctrinal statements are themselves an insufficient guard against spiritual error. There have been institutions that signed the same doctrinal statement but in reality believed and practiced differently. Much religious belief and practice has been aligned, to take but two examples, with the Anglican Thirty-Nine Articles or the Presbyterian Westminster Catechism. Both confessions are fine examples of doctrinal statements, and important creedal affirmations.

But it is possible to have organizations apparently defined by one or other of these doctrinal statements whose heart is far from their intention and whose fruit is not that of the Holy Spirit. These institutions interpret these doctrinal statements by the letter, perhaps, and not the spirit. Or they sign them with fingers crossed behind their back. Or they simply misunderstand them. Or, even more commonly, some new defining doctrinal issue emerges that neither of these historic creeds addresses. Worthy and wonderful as those doctrinal statements were, nowadays, without something in addition, they can become worse than useless: they can become dangerous, talismans of orthodoxy, when really, because of the changing times, they no longer protect Christians from heresy. Our spiritual boat needs to avoid new rocks, and, without new lighthouses warning us, if we focus only on the old, we end up ship-wrecked on the new.

So doctrinal statements are not enough. One approach to these problems is to update our doctrinal statements continually to deal with emerging new challenges to the Christian faith, as church history shows churches have always done. It is important to do so, for it guards us against certain kinds of error.

But it is not enough to have the letter of orthodoxy yet not the spirit. It is not enough to honor the law but not love the Lord. Otherwise we end up with phylacteries wide but hearts narrow and bitter. If we just focus on the doctrinal, we become nothing more than Pharisees, or even liberals, unwittingly swallowing the hook, line and sinker of a new error because we have not learnt to discern spiritually: we can discern only methodically and mechanically. We have, as one old Christian leader I knew complained of the rising generation of Christian leaders, no "sense of smell" about new Christian movements, fads, fashions or teaching.

Edwards aims to teach us this subtle, important matter of discerning spiritually. Of fundamental and foundational importance, it goes to the heart of how we know we are saved, how we know what we believe is true, and therefore how we know we are on track to heaven and not hell. Nothing could be more important.

SPIRITUALITY IS DIAGNOSED BY 'FRUIT'

Edwards' approach is in essence simple. It is a straightforward application of an utterly clear biblical teaching. Jesus warns us that to tell true from false teachers we must apply a simple principle: discern them by their fruit. The passage in the Bible is worth quoting in full, for it stands behind everything Edwards says:

> Watch out for false prophets. They come to you in sheep's clothing, but inwardly they are ferocious wolves. By their fruit you will recognize them. Do people pick grapes from thorn bushes, or figs from thistles? Likewise every good tree bears good fruit, but a bad tree bears bad fruit. A good tree cannot bear bad fruit, and a bad tree cannot bear good fruit. Every tree that does not bear good fruit is cut down and thrown into the fire. Thus, by their fruit you will recognize them. (Matthew 7:15–20)

This is all Edwards is saying. Following Jesus, Edwards does not point us to what the false teachers are saying. Of course that is important. In other places the Bible does tell us to look at what people teach as a way to discern whether someone is from God or not. John tells us not to listen to anyone who does not say what the apostles are saying (1 John 4:6). The apostle Paul tells the Corinthians that prophets must obey his apostolic teaching, or they will be ignored (1 Corinthians 14:37–38). Yes, we must discern *doctrinally*. But there is an as important, more subtle yet ultimately as significant, kind of determination: *fruit*.

It is with this that Edwards is concerned. It is not *what* they teach. Why not? Because the very worst kind of teaching sounds just fine. Haven't we all experienced that? False teachers of the worst kind will sign anything and say anything to get among the sheep. They are in sheep's clothing. They intend to sound orthodox. So the doctrinal test alone will not do. We need a more acute test.

Edwards here comes into his own. We all understand we need to follow Jesus' teaching about discerning by fruit, but many of us are unsure what it means to do so. In Edwards' day people looked at the revival and said, well they seem to be teaching the truth, so that's good, but look at how they're going about it. It's all new. There are novelties. There is disorder. They're doing it the wrong way. It's not what they're doing; it's *how* they're doing it, the process, pattern and method that are wrong. Therefore both they and this revival must be wrong. It is of the devil, and we will not, no must not – for fear of our eternal soul – listen to it.

All the while during the Great Awakening many people were being converted, but because it was done in a new *way* others rejected it. Edwards wanted to stand against that attitude and say, no, that's wrong. You've got to remember what Jesus said. He didn't say you can tell them by the way the tree grows, or the angle of the branches. No, it's all about the fruit.

That is all Edwards is saying. But it is profoundly and fundamentally important. If we miss it, we miss everything, God's great blessing for us. We may reject something we should accept, or accept something we should reject. Furthermore, we may not just miss out on a blessing; we may place ourselves on the broad road that leads to destruction.

So, according to Edwards, what matters is not only what a new Christian movement's teachers say (though that is important), but the results of its spiritual experience. If the devil is being defeated, if people are being saved, if the gospel is progressing, then a movement must be of God.

This focus upon the fruit is the essence of what Edwards is saying. However, there are innumerable pitfalls to avoid and, again, Edwards helps enormously.

EDWARDS' SEVEN KEY PRINCIPLES

Seven key principles of testing by fruit run throughout his various writings on the matter. His principles are applied in *The Distinguishing Marks* and then in a fuller and more profound version in *The Religious Affections*. The same approach appears in his other sermons and writings on the matter.

1. Negative signs

Many things are not signs of whether or not an experience or new movement is of God. Edwards seemed to feel that discovering and understanding these non-signs is just as valuable as discovering the signs. This derived from Edwards' view of the work of God and of the substance of human nature. Edwards considered the non-signs especially important because we often misjudge on the basis of things that are not signs.

For instance, Edwards argued that the fact that something is done in an unusual way, or by an extraordinary method, does not tell us whether it is of God or not of God. He said, "There is a great aptness in persons to doubt of things that are strange; especially in elderly persons," and remarked that "if it be a good argument that a work is not from the Spirit of God, that it is very unusual, then it was so in the apostles' day. The work of the Spirit, then, was carried on in a manner that, in very many respects, was altogether new" (E. Hickman [ed.], *The Works of Jonathan Edwards* [Banner of Truth], 1988, vol. 2, p. 261).

If the method is new, that does not mean it is of God, nor does it mean it is not of God. The method does not tell us one way or another. Edwards made the same point with physical manifestations. Much time has been wasted discussing the physical manifestations of this or that new Christian movement. Edwards simply said they are immaterial, for they do not tell us one way or the other whether or not something is of God. So he said:

> A work is not to be judged of by any effects on the bodies of men; such as tears, trembling, groans, loud outcries, agonies of body, or the failing of body strength . . . We cannot conclude that persons are under the influence of the true Spirit because we see such effects upon their bodies, because this is not given as a mark of the true Spirit; nor on the other hand, have we any reason to conclude, from such outward appearances, that persons are not under the influence of the Spirit of God, because there is no rule of Scripture given us to judge of spirits by, that does either expressly or indirectly exclude such effects on the body, nor does reason exclude them. (Hickman, *Works of Jonathan Edwards*, vol. 2, p. 261)

Physical effects also do not decide the matter one way or another.

Edwards listed many similar "negative signs." They are physical or circumstantial aspects of a movement or experience that may be striking or remarkable, but for the purposes of discernment are simply immaterial; they do not tell one way or another whether or not something is of God.

2. Spiritual origin

After these various negative signs, Edwards, in both *The Religious Affections* and *The Distinguishing Marks,* described positive signs. In these positive signs he applied the key principle that they are all of spiritual origin. Positive signs are what the devil either cannot or will not do, are beyond human capacity to imitate, and therefore must be God at work. "There are some of these things that the devil would not do if he could . . . and there are other things that the devil neither can nor will do." When a movement functions to convict people of sin and awaken the conscience, it must be of God, for this "operates against the interests of Satan's kingdom, which lies in encouraging and establishing sin, and cherishing men's worldly lusts" (Hickman, *Works of Jonathan Edwards,* vol. 2, p. 269). The positive signs are so judicious because they evidence a movement's true spiritual origin.

3. New sense

One of the key positive signs, therefore, is the new sense given to those who genuinely experience the work of God. Edwards discusses this at length in *The Religious Affections:*

> So that the spiritual perceptions which a sanctified and spiritual
> person has are [as different] as the ideas and sensations of different
> senses do differ. Hence the work of the Spirit of God in regeneration
> is often in Scripture compared to the giving a new sense, giving eyes
> to see, and ears to hear, unstopping the ears of the deaf, and opening
> the eyes of them that were born blind, and turning from darkness
> unto light.
> (J. E. Smith, H. S. Stout and K. P. Minkema [eds.], *A Jonathan
> Edwards Reader* [Yale University Press, 1995], p. 161)

This is the "sense of the heart" we discussed in the previous chapter. The "sense of the heart" was also a sign. The enjoyment, appreciation and relish of spiritual things was a distinguishing mark, fruit or sign of being truly spiritual.

4. Esteeming truth

Edwards proposed that a growing esteem for the truth is an evidence of a true Christian movement or experience. "When the operation," or spiritual movement or experience, "is such as to raise their esteem of that Jesus who was born of the Virgin, and was crucified without the gates of Jerusalem," when it causes "a greater regard to the Holy Scriptures," when the experience is "convincing them of those things that are true, we may safely determine that it is a right and true spirit" (Hickman, *Works of Jonathan Edwards*, vol. 2, pp. 266–268).

By the "truth" he means such things as "that there is a God," "that he is a great and sin-hating God," "that life is short, and uncertain," "that there is another world" and that we "must give account of [ourselves] to God" (*Distinguishing Marks*). Attraction to the truth of God's Word is a clear distinguishing mark of the spiritual origin of a movement.

5. Humble love

The ultimate sign for Edwards was not esteeming truth, but humble love. In this way he was merely reflecting the teaching of Jesus that "all men will know that you are my disciples if you love one another" (John 13:35), and that love is the greatest commandment (Matthew 22:37–40). Love is the pre-eminent Christian ethic. Edwards understood that love can be faked. We can have societies that appear to care for each other but just have a selfish kind of "you scratch my back and I'll scratch yours" mutual support. What makes the self-orientated social network different from true Christian love? "The surest character of true divine supernatural love . . . is, that the Christian virtue of *humility* shines in it; that which above all others renounces, abases, and annihilates what we term self" (Hickman, *Works of Jonathan Edwards*, vol. 2, p. 268).

81

6. Discernment, not judgment

None of these signs, marks or "fruit," Edwards carefully clarified, were intended to enable us to be the certain and capable judges of another person's heart. One problem that emerged during the Great Awakening was that some radically took the movement to an extreme and started declaring publicly and definitively who was and who was not saved on the basis of flimsy evidence and with arrogant presumption. Edwards was clear that he was not attempting to be judgmental or encourage presumptuous judging of others. If he was going to do that, he said, "I should be guilty of that arrogance which I have been condemning" (Smith, Stout and Minkema, *Jonathan Edwards Reader*, p. 153). What was the point of these signs, then, if not to judge? Edwards felt that, while we may not know for sure who are really saved and who are not, the Bible gives us "rules" or standards by which we may guide ourselves and our churches towards truth and away from error. The ultimate judgment between the sheep and the goats is God's business and he will "reserve this to himself" (ibid., p. 154). We have a responsibility to discern, not judge.

7. Passion not passivity

Edwards wanted to provide a series of tests that would on the one hand prevent us from being gullible, but also on the other hand enable us to join with new Christian movements and endeavors without forever waiting on the sidelines and wondering whether this or that is "of God" or not. There is a great and grand call to action in *The Distinguishing Marks*. Edwards concluded that the Great Awakening was, in general, "undoubtedly" of the Spirit of God. He warned people, therefore, not to oppose the work of God, or to be silent about it. Such a silence, especially from ministers, was "provoking to God." This he said was a "pretended prudence," but would "probably in them prove the greatest imprudence' because they would miss "the most precious opportunity of obtaining divine light, grace, and comfort, heavenly and eternal blessings, that God ever gave in New England" (Hickman, *Works of Jonathan Edwards*, vol.

2, p. 273). Edwards' signs were intended to equip us to make accurate decisions and thereafter become passionately involved.

APPLYING THE PRINCIPLES TODAY

These seven principles underlay Edwards' extensive discussion of discerning new Christian movements. His signs were discriminating without being judgmental, careful without being passive, passionate without being fractious and, above all, thoroughly biblical. Edwards did not merely identify these biblical principles; he applied them acutely to the human soul. We need to do the same with the new Christian movements, developments, ideas and attitudes flooding the world. It is not enough to have the principles. We must do the work prayerfully to consider how they apply to the questions that face us. How do we assess these new Christian movements? Are they of God in general? Are they not of God? What should be our attitude and action, depending on what conclusion we come to?

To begin with, we have to ask what kind of new Christian movements we are talking about. What is new for someone may be old to someone else. We could immediately think of the controversial matters in church life, which must have been around for long enough to become controversial, for different parties and groups to have been solidified in opposition to or in support of the "new" Christian movement. Nonetheless, because these matters are controversial we understandably look to someone like Edwards to provide guidance about them. How would Edwards assess the burgeoning growth in the last hundred years of Christian churches that have emphasized the miraculous gifts of the Spirit? What would Edwards think of the church-growth movement? Would Edwards have an opinion about ecumenicism, or about less controversial modern matters?

In many parts of the non-Western world Christianity is booming. Near where I work, in New Haven in the United States, is an Overseas Ministries Study Center. We occasionally have one of their residents teach a Bible class or give a sermon. We find out that this or that person is a pastor of, say, a ten-thousand-member church and in charge of a group of churches throughout an enormous region, all substantially larger than your average church in North America, let alone Britain. This is obviously "new" to a large extent, and much of the academic "missionary" literature predicts a global shift in Christianity from North to South. What are we to make of it? These questions are too large to answer satisfactorily or cogently. After all, which kind of "charismatic" church are we talking about? They are not all the same, any more than every Baptist or Anglican church is the same. What area of the world or what part of the emerging new "global" church are we discussing? What sort of church-growth emphasis do we mean? In all this there will be innumerable local variations. In many ways it is more important, then, to be able to apply these tests concretely. The more weighty question is not "What am I to make of this or that global emphasis?" but "What about this church down the road?" Should I join that church or another church? It is less significant to have a vague opinion on some tendency in Christian publishing than to know the right answer to the question "What am I to think of this book that a friend has lent me?" Is it sound, heretical or just plain woolly? When we think of "new Christian movements," we need to approach the matter concretely. It is more helpful to know what to think about a particular influential group who gather together nearby than it is to have some masterful dissertation on an international comintern. The really important questions are, "Am I to get involved? Should I stay away? Should I believe this? Should I support that?"

This means the vital skill to develop is learning how to apply biblical tests ourselves. Although we may wish it, the Bible does not give us an eternal list of "sound" and "unsound" churches. Instead it gives us a series of principles we need to apply. The apostle John in particular urges Christians to apply these, to be active in discerning. Perhaps the most significant take-home message from Edwards' list of tests is that we must test. So John says, "But you have an anointing from the Holy One, and all of you know the truth" (1 John 2:20) and therefore "test the spirits to see whether they are from God" (1 John 4:1). He is writing to normal Christians. He wants them to test and expects them to do so. They have the truth and need to apply it to divide the true from the false. I want to suggest two ways we can make Edwards' series of tests concrete. They apply to our attempts to deal with cultural change in the West, and to our fractured opinions about charismatic gifts. We are immersed in a time of great cultural change and no longer live in the "Christian West."

That is certainly true in Europe, increasingly true in Britain, and becoming true in North America. This secularization is the fundamental issue of change that affects the Christian church. People talk about it in various intellectual and philosophical ways, but the bottom-line issue for Christian mission is that the culture in general no longer accepts the claims of Christ to be the Savior of the world.

How are we to respond? There are many theories out there, but for simplicity's sake they may be characterized into two groups: those who always initiate and change to meet the changes, and those who feel that what is required is to maintain a more traditional style. Which of these approaches is more effective? It is not easy to say. Sometimes traditional groups can be quite innovative, whereas "contemporary" groups can simply ape what appears to be the latest fashion among Christians rather than what is most helpful in reaching out to non-Christians. How do we assess these approaches?

Edwards' description of the missionary David Brainerd helps here. He explains how Brainerd passionately sought the conversion of the Native American Indians. He describes the success he achieved. Brainerd did not abandon the message. In fact, Brainerd emphasized conviction of sin and repentance. But Brainerd did go to "live" with the people, and inhabit the indigenous groups in a bold, passionate and committed way. It is this missionary model that it is necessary for us to understand in our current culture change. We need to see ourselves as culture missionaries, inhabiting the culture within which we live, a part of it in some respects, but bringing a radically different message and way of living to it at the same time. This is not "compromise" with the world, for, if that were the case, then God the Son's incarnation was a compromise. No, it was not compromise but sacrifice, a leaving behind of the familiar to take up the burden of reaching the lost.

This is essential. People today, even in the secular West, have a "sense" of God, of the transcendent, of the divine. We need to tap into that with the message of the gospel.

How do we assess which approach is working? By the "fruit." This does not mean simply that the largest church is the best. This could be a delusion, just bringing the world into the church. It means questions of a more subtle nature about the love for each other evidenced in such movements, about the passionate desire for truth, about the humility and Christian character being produced. The fruit is what counts: not the gifts or the numbers, but the character of those involved. What is that like? And as soon as we ask that, we find we have help with the next foundationally important issue of assessment for the Christian church today: our fractured opinions about the charismatic gifts.

Edwards was not, as I have already mentioned, a charismatic. He believed in the cessation of gifts. He spoke in fiery terms against those who thought God was talking to them in some direct-impression kind of way. However, when it came to testing spiritual experience, Edwards employed fruit as his category of analysis. The theology of gifts is a doctrinal matter of weight. But for Edwards they were not a sufficient *test*. They may be one test, yes, but they are not a sufficient *test*. Are we really willing to say that whatever someone believes about the charismatic gifts is really a test of whether that person is saved or not? Whether God is using them or not? Whether there is anything good in the movement or not? Is our opinion about the gifts what saves us? What matters more are the results of Christian character.

We need a real-world or real-church assessment of the fruit of the Spirit in Christian character. Is this movement producing a greater relish for Christian truth? If it is not, it cannot be of God, for he wishes us to know the truth, which will set us free. It is Satan who has no interest in truth but only in lies. Is this movement producing spiritual humility and love? Or is it producing overweening pride that suggests "we" are the superspiritual ones, the spiritual elite, chosen by heaven for God's favor?

If it produces that kind of attitude, whatever the theological niceties, the spirit at work in that movement cannot be God's Spirit. For God's Spirit produces the character of the Beatitudes: meekness, gentleness, self-control, love and kindness. It does not produce the character of the boastful. We must apply the principle Jesus himself gave us when he said we would know them by their fruit.

Now the only other thing to realize is how radical Edwards' assessment criteria were at the time he fashioned them. There were, as we saw in chapter 2, the "Old Lights." These gradually moved further and further "left," until they ended in what we would call liberalism, and in some cases total unitarianism, where they no longer believed in the Trinity. Then, on the other extreme, were the "New Lights." Edwards was one of these, though he was what we could call a "moderate New Light," for some of the new lights became the worst enemies of the Great Awakening even while they aimed to be its best friends. They took things to an extreme and became judgmental. Edwards' assessments were radical in that he put his reputation and weight fully behind the revival, even though he knew that not everything about the revival was correct.

What is so amazing about that? Well, many of us would tend to wait until we found something "wholly of God." Or if we found something partly good, we would lend it our partial support. Edwards was not like that. Why? It goes back to his understanding of how the Holy Spirit works with humans. Because we are humans, because we are flesh and blood, and because we are fallen humans, we are sinful; even the greatest work of God in history will be tainted by human failing and sinful behavior. It must be like that. Why? Because God is working with sinful humans. That does not make him the author of sin. But if God's Spirit comes upon a sinful human, there will be human results and there may even be sinful results. If I am powerfully moved by God, I may weep, cry, jump up and down. It would be surprising if I did nothing after a powerful encounter with the living Lord Jesus! Then, though, depending on my constitution and maturity, I may also take these to an extreme. I may become part of a movement that emphasizes leaping up and down as a sign, not just a potential and immaterial by-product, of God's work. That is wrong, but it doesn't make the experience wrong. It just means my judgment is wrong, and my humanity is getting involved. Or I may begin to denounce anyone who does not jump up and down. That again does not make my original experience unwarranted; it just means my unsanctified pride is masking itself in religious behavior, and religious pride is the trickiest of failings to heal. Jesus, after all, was opposed by the Pharisees.

So mixed blessings are always present, even in true revival. That must be the case, because humans are being revived. The mixed results can happen in some of the ways I have just mentioned, or in any number of other ways. But, in a sense, so what? The mixed nature of the matter does not deny God was at work originally. If God produces in this movement a great longing for Scripture and a love for the truth of God, the Bible, Jesus and the atonement, if there is humility and love, Christian character in all its Christ-like glory, then the movement is of God. And I should not embrace it half-heartedly or partially, but passionately and fervently, working hard to remove the movement's failings, and fanning into flame that which is purely of God.

If I wait for a work of God to come with no attendant failings, then I wait for heaven. Which is right in its own way, but I will miss out on great blessings, and many people, under God's providence, may not have a chance to hear the gospel and be saved. I should get involved and be a part of shaping the movement to better ends with better means.

So how do we avoid throwing out the baby with the bathwater? We focus on the baby, not the bathwater. We focus on Christ and on the fruit of the Spirit – and if there is dirty bathwater, we throw it out.

5.

THE CAUSE OF MODERNISM'S PLIGHT IS ITS HUMAN-CENTEREDNESS

Two middle-aged men are on stage discussing topics of mundane importance. They appear to be waiting. Sure enough they start talking about someone they are expecting. They wonder when he will arrive. They keep on talking. They sit down. They stand. Nothing happens. They wait. Finally they decide Godot is not coming to meet them. They say they had better leave. They never move. The curtain falls with them remaining exactly where they were. Hardly a Hollywood blockbuster, but Samuel Becket's *Waiting for Godot* has become an epitome of the criticisms of modern life. Godot, of course, is God, and *Waiting for Godot* tells us there is no point waiting for God to show up. In a lighter vein, *The Wizard of Oz* may imply the same thing. There is no wizard, just a funny little man behind a curtain pulling levers. God is dead, the message goes, and modern people need to grow up and learn to live with it.

WHAT IS WRONG WITH THE MODERN WORLD?

You may not think the modern world is in any kind of plight. After all, there have been innumerable advances over the last hundred years, and in many ways life has changed incontrovertibly for the better. We now have motor cars, no longer horse-drawn carriages. We have airplanes. We have space ships. Economic development in the modernized world has outstripped all predictions, giving unparalleled wealth and opportunity to a far greater proportion of people than was true in pre-industrial civilizations. We have the Internet, email, the ubiquitous mobile phone. We also have fast food, relatively cheap fine dining, cinemas, videos, DVDs, computer games. We have a "safety net" of social support for those who fall through the cracks. We have medical advances that achieve wonders every day undreamt of a mere half-century ago. We have educational and scientific advances. We have entertainment on a vast scale.

As the list goes on we begin to sense the dark side of modern life as well. This has given rise to the global popularistic outcry against many of the trammels of modernity, like the World Bank and the G8 Summits. People are protesting that something has gone wrong. For, while there have been unparalleled gains for a few, a larger group than before, the gains have come at considerable cost to other aspects of life. The developing world is advancing, yet people starve in one corner of the globe while in another a mountain of food grows ever higher. What is more, while modern societies themselves are remarkable places, they are hardly havens of righteousness or beacons of light. Rampant sexuality vies with sexually transmitted diseases, until some estimate that one in five Americans over the age of 12 has contracted a sexually transmitted disease. AIDS may not yet have caused the devastation predicted in the Western world, but in Africa and elsewhere the death toll and horror mount.

Then there are the more subtle issues, the sense of *ennui*, of meaninglessness, of the cost of disassociation from family that the demands of a fast-paced economy make upon the relational structures that enrich life. If my family lives thousands of miles from me, in what sense am I being enriched? Materially, perhaps, but relationally? Or spiritually? In fact it is this sense of "spirit" that sensitive commentators have noticed as most obviously lacking from the basic philosophy and experience of "modernity." Where is the "ghost in the machine," the sense of transcendence and awe that makes life magical? Against all these and more the counter-culture protests when it marches against the establishment. Yet it often does so with a lack of appreciation for the enormous gains of modernity, which the protestors rely upon when they go to a super-market or public toilet, or are rushed to hospital. Modern life has indeed produced great gains, from the industrial revolution to the exponential advance of science, from the post-industrial service-driven economy to the Internet and email, and so on. Yet at the same time there is a sense something is missing. Some of the negatives are far from hidden – the crime, disease, immorality and waste of modern life are there for all to see. Some of them are equally, if not more, pervasive but take reflec-tion to spot. Is the high divorce rate due to a lowering commitment to marriage as an institution? That seems unlikely, given that society still seems to have an "and they live happily ever after" dream. Or are the divorce courts packed because modern life exerts such pressure on the dual-income family that marriage becomes exceptionally hard work to sustain? We might also wonder about the growing levels of depression in modern life. Are they due to the soullessness of modern life that generates hopelessness? We could wonder equally about sexuality and sexually transmitted diseases. Is a sexually rampant society fuelled by simple freedom? Or is the individualism, the possibility for people to commute, "do their own thing," live on their own in the big city, so necessary to a modernized economy, something that almost inevitably generates increasing frequency of "hooking up" without a commitment to the long term – for who knows what or where the long term will be?

Modern life does have a dark side, but what is its cause? Many com-mentators these days assert that the cause of modernism's bad effects is its totalitizing tendency. Modernism tends, such views hold, to create an attitude to life that assumes its ways of acting, believing and thinking are the only appropriate ways of being. Such an ideology is, inevitably, repressive and tends to victimize those it opposes, in other countries or in the counter-culture at home. It becomes lacking in tolerance and represses the spirit. The alternative, such people would assert, is to generate a culture with a more generous, pluralistic and ideologically relativistic world view. By this they mean it would assume all religions, creeds and lifestyles are acceptable.

WHAT EDWARDS WOULD SAY ABOUT THE MODERN WORLD

Edwards' critique of modernity would be its foundational lack of God-centeredness: that you have the wrong god, or no god, or the true God is sidelined. In his view, life, reality, existence, and therefore all sustainable prosperity and social interaction of whatever kind, are founded upon God, rely upon him and must be given to him as an act of worship. That is, life must be foundationally God-centered. Or, even more, *thoroughly* God-centered; it is not just about beginning with God (foundationally God-centered), but about having a God-centered view of life influencing all our thinking, feeling, believing and acting.

Of course, Edwards never addressed a G8 Summit, but if he had, it might have gone something like this: "You are pleased with your economic development. You have worked hard at applying what you feel are the laws of a free-market economy. But your freedom will never be free unless you acknowledge, worship and let rule the true invisible hand of the market, of life, and of all reality: God Himself." He would have said, "God is in charge! God is God! Worship him! Bow down to him! Obey him! Do not worship money or power – or even the postmodern idea that there is no truth at all, for that itself is a form of worship. No; instead, worship God!"

There are four main sources of this God-centered approach in Edwards' writings. In a sense, all of Edwards' writings were God-centered, as he argued that all life (and therefore writing and preaching) needed to be God-centered. In particular, however, Edwards advanced his God-centered view of life in four areas of his ministry. The first was in his preaching. Edwards was foremost a preacher and his sermons are foundationally God-centered.

The second source of his God-centeredness is found in a book called *The Freedom of the Will.* Terms about the will are notoriously slippery in philosophical discussion, and Edwards' famous dissertation on the freedom of the will was really arguing the same basic point about human willing that Martin Luther did in his book *The Bondage of the Will.* Edwards chose a different title, and different mode of arguing, partly because of his approach to human freedom – which, as we shall see, relied upon our God-centeredness.

The third area was Edwards' book *The End for Which God Created the World.* Edwards' answer to the question "Why did God create the world?" was simply "For his own glory." This may seem an obvious answer. Yet when we think about it, as Edwards' book forces us to do, and consider what it means and what the ramifications are or should be of that belief, in our everyday lives, the implications are enormous: I am not here for myself, but for God.

The final main artery through which Edwards' concept of the God-centeredness of life flowed was Edwards' voluminous unpublished writing. These notes covered an exhaustive array of subjects. By no means all discussed specifically the God-centeredness of life. But these notes are an especially useful source for working out how Edwards' God-centeredness applies to such a wide range of issues, ideas and subjects.

Each of these avenues of information contributes something to our understanding of Edwards' view of life as "theocentric" or God-centered. They tell us that Edwards considered life best viewed as God-centered in respect of our decision-making, destiny, ministry and intellectual apparatus and framework. Edwards' explicit and meticulously phrased descriptions of the profound God-centeredness of life were not in an ideological vacuum. He viewed this God-centeredness as the antidote to the emerging materialistic, relativistic and humanistic strains within the Enlightenment. As such it may not be so big a historical leap, in some sense, to imagine him addressing a G8 Summit, modern university campus, scientific conference, or counseling training session. Edwards' theocentricism is a coordinated response to a malignant tendency in modern life to go spiritually and pragmatically astray. Here is how he does it.

Edwards' God-centered view of life explained

First, Edwards viewed human willing as inevitably and truly God-centered. This was most apparent in *The Freedom of the Will.* The book is one of the masterpieces of philosophical theology (or, as it might perhaps in some ways be better described, theological philosophy). It is a complex book with many complex and carefully interwoven and finely tuned arguments. Basically, Edwards argued, God gives us freedom. As a good Calvinist, Edwards believed that everything we think, do or say is in some sense ultimately and completely under the sovereign rule of the Almighty. Yet he termed his dissertation on the subject *The Freedom of the Will.* As mentioned earlier, Edwards was actually making the same point as Martin Luther's thesis, *The Bondage of the Will.* Two very different titles describing the same theological point. What is going on?

Edwards was attempting to refute a false notion of the will that was gaining momentum. That view was that humans are themselves sovereign over their own decision-making. They are in charge. Edwards did not argue a kind of fatalistic philosophy in response. It is true he knew that his doctrine was similar, in some ways, to that of Thomas Hobbes, a famous contemporary fatalistic philosopher. But Hobbes, as Edwards said, had made bad use of the idea. Edwards' approach was different. He argued that all humans are free to decide. I decide what I am going to do in the morning, what I am going to eat for breakfast, who I am going to marry, and so on. I am, in this apparent and self-evident way, free. However, Edwards argued, while I am free to decide, I decide upon the basis of what I like, what I appreciate, what I enjoy, what I esteem, what I hold to be important or worthy. I am free, Edwards would say, to choose what I like but I am not free to like what I choose. My taste is set by various matters, we could speculate. It may be set by my parents and their upbringing. It may be set by my genetic code. It may be set by my environment or various events that have happened to me. I am still a thinking, choosing, willing being in the middle of these factors, but they have an influence upon me.

Edwards argued that behind all these various influences, surrounding them, in them, and through them, was the will of God. In other words, God gives us freedom. The significance of God's sovereignty is terribly important to appreciate today. We are in the midst of many debates about how free we really are. Genetic advances have exposed the extent of our "hard-wired" apparatus. Sociological studies have documented the profound influence environment has upon our choices. Behaviorists analyze these matters and developmental theories predict each stage of our lives. But our much-vaunted human freedom is really an illusion. The film *The Truman Show* or the series *The Matrix* is at least partly about this: we feel we are making decisions, living our lives as we choose, but the truth is, we are in a web of connected experiences or other influences that control our lives and destiny.

In *The Freedom of the Will*, the point is that humans are really only ever truly free when they submit to the will of God. This is a basic discipleship point, but it needs to be pressed in our current environment as a matter of first importance. It is a lie that we are free without God. We are merely slaves to our whims, which are set by our genetic make-up, our environment, even our parents. Only God's will, and the personal assertion of faith in God's will, only his involvement and our trust in that, can transform our macabre "matrix" into a masterful display of God's glory and genuine freedom.

Not only, though, did Edwards view human decision-making as God-centered; he understood our destiny as God-centered. This came out most clearly in his book *The End for which God Created the World*. In that book Edwards made the simple point that the questions we all ask about the meaning of life can be answered satisfyingly by realizing I am not the center of the universe, but God is. 'Why am I here?' we ask. "What is my purpose? What should I be doing? Where should I be going?" All these questions about destiny and purpose are biblically, and only satisfyingly, answered by the belief in God's glory being the end of all existence. This may seem selfish on the part of God, but, as the Creator, only he is the center of everything. His self can be the center and not be damaging to other selves. He is the rightful heir and ruler. When we focus on our selves, we are narrowly selfish; when God is glorified, the universe vibrates with a wonder and beauty too awesome to be described.

Again, this approach is crucial. All that "soul searching" and trying to find "meaning" and "purpose" is rightly and truly satisfied only when we turn our attention away from ourselves and focus on God. I am confused about who I am because I think about myself more than I think about God. It is only in *him* that I find my true orientation. That sense of meandering, pointlessness and fatigue derives from the same central issue. It is not about me, but about God. Seeing that makes my life wake up and move from practicing off-tune scales to playing with the divine orchestra. I am a part of something larger than life. I am made for worship. Anything less disappoints. We could go on, but this central point of The *End for which God Created the World* is forgotten at our spiritual and psychological peril, and relished to our great good and joy.

Whereas Edwards' preaching functions as a standard of God-centered ministry, much of our ministry is driven not by the Word, and therefore not by the Lord, but rather by the expectations of our audience. We become caterers, not proclaimers. We develop a menu to please all palates, but because of the structure, style and approach the implicit message becomes fundamentally and foundationally human-centered. We are concerned to please rather than win our hearers. This temptation is common to all in ministry, for we want success. There is also a need for careful balance. For while we are not called to preach in a way that panders to the itching ears of our congregations, we are called to "persuade" and be an "ambassador," and these require appealing and diplomatic words and an approach conducive to gaining a hearing.

Edwards' preaching, however, was thoroughly God-centered. This does not mean he gave no practical direction, though. Often the largest segment of his sermon was practical application to everyday life. Here is one sermon at random as an example:

Hence we may solve the difficulty of some Christians meeting with so much affliction and darkness in the world . . . If their happiness throughout all eternity be so great, of how little consequence is it what may be their condition for that short moment they continue in this world! What if they are in the dark, what if they walk in darkness and are exercised with great trouble! How little difference will it make, though it be cast into the scales, when weighed against that far more exceeding and eternal weight of glory! It will prove lighter than vanity. (Preached December 1740 on Romans 2:10; unpublished manuscript)

Edwards is here preaching on the glory of heaven. He spends an extensive part of the sermon describing in emotive and concrete theological terms the reality wonder of the experience of heaven preaching enables him to for the redeemed. Then he comes, in classic Puritan sermon mode, to the "application" or "use" of the questions in a profoundly sermon. Here we find the real bite of such God-centeredness, of focusing the attention of the sermon on God's agenda. He deals with that matter of trouble for so many: suffering. He approaches and tackles it. Once he has established the foundation of looking at things through God's eyes, the subject is relatively easily handled. "If this is what heaven is like," Edwards in effect says, "then while suffering is like this, and does occur, even among the righteous, yet it is of no account in the scales because the weight of glory, eternal glory, outweighs its considerations, as the pain of inoculation against a terminal illness is outweighed by the health it guarantees. Even more so: there is not just a lack of pain or trouble; there is an eternal gift of joy and glory."

Not only did Edwards' preaching function as a standard of God-centeredness, not only did his approach to human destiny aid our psychological and spiritual need for purpose by orientating those desires around God-centeredness, not only did his argument about human freedom establish our freedom on the basis of God's total sovereignty, but he also brought to our world view an intellectual framework that was thoroughly God-centered.

Edwards viewed all of reality, existence, life, both spiritual and physical, constantly and continually as dependent for its sustenance upon the active perception of God. We find this throughout his voluminous, carefully crafted private notes. Despite what some once thought, Edwards did not lay aside his philosophical speculations after he was converted or went into the ministry. His philosophical ruminations were part and parcel of his most practical ministry: fuel to the fire. They were the framework out of which his specific directions and pastoral counsel came.

Edwards believed in what scholars have termed "continuous creation": the idea that not only did God create the world, not only does he sustain it, but the world is, as it were, constantly created anew every moment by God's willing, action and perception. This perception was the key. Edwards lived at a time when the materialistic element of the Enlightenment was beginning to be forced by, in particular, the materialistic philosophy of Thomas Hobbes. Edwards' view of God-centeredness was viewed in contradistinction to Hobbes. He also lived at a time when, at the other extreme, the empirical emphasis of John Locke and the early scientists was beginning to lead to a place where all was relative to our perceptions. Radical skepticism, in the form of doubting what we could know or be sure of knowing, was just down the road. This was foreshadowed in the work of idealist philosopher George Berkeley, who viewed all of life, in some way or other, as an idea.

Edwards countered both the stagnant materialism of Hobbes and the vibrant but relativistic idealism of Berkeley through his view of all of reality being based on God's continual activity and constant perception.

It is this view of God's immediate presence – when developed thus in terms of our existing because we are perceived by God – that gave so much weight to the horror of Edwards' descriptions of our sins. Sin is not just the creature sinning against the Creator; it is the creature in constant dependence for every breath upon the Sovereign Lord, but using that breath instead to curse his God. There is an immediacy to Edwards' preaching and ministry that is a practical expression of his concept of our total and immediate dependence upon God. "'Tis certain with me,"

Edwards writes in number 125a of his *Miscellanies*, "that the world exists anew every moment." He carries on, "Indeed, we every moment see the same proof of a God as we should have seen, if we had seen [him] create the world at first. Rev. 4:11, 'For thy pleasure they are and were created.'" For Edwards, "no matter is, in the most proper sense, matter," and matter "is truly nothing at all, strictly and in itself considered" (Miller, Smith and Stout, "Things to be Considered," *The Works of Jonathan Edwards*, vol. 6, pp. 235, 238). By such a seemingly strange description of matter, he meant that the concept of an independent material "substance" supporting the universe is incorrect; actually, he argued in corollary number 11 in his note "On Atoms," "speaking most strictly, there is no proper substance but God himself" (P. Miller, J. E. Smith and H. S. Stout [eds.], *The Works of Jonathan Edwards* [Yale University Press, 1957–2004], vol. 6, p. 215).

All this was intended to get away from the view of the world as a "machine," in response to which Christians either celebrate God as the Grand Engineer or find a "gap" in the machine where they may assert evidence for the existence of God. Both Isaac Newton and John Locke attempted this "god of the gaps" approach: Newton argued gravity evidenced God's existence, while Locke said human consciousness did.

Edwards took a different course. Others simply welcomed the new science of the Enlightenment and celebrated God as its author, as the Puritan Cotton Mather did in his "The Christian Philosopher". Edwards, though, while also welcoming many aspects of the new science and the Enlightenment, founded the whole venture on a view of God that was far more immediate and all-consuming. This, he acknowledged in corollary number 34, "The Mind," made no difference to the practical life of work or the practice of science. Instead it was intended to make an enormous difference to how we felt about God and considered him. Edwards' radically God-centered view of life, existence and all of reality ensured a view of God in which God could be asserted as immediately present, without having to scrape around for a bit of reality that science had not yet explained. The whole thing was God's. Edwards discussed this in different ways. In particular his concept of beauty was an attempt to shore up the objectivity of reality in a way that could be subjectively appropriated.

WHAT IS THE DIFFERENCE BETWEEN BEING HUMAN-CENTERED AND GOD-CENTERED?

The best way to understand the kind of thing Edwards was proposing in this way, and through his writing and preaching at a more accessible level, is to compare how a "human-centered" view influences our experience of life with how a more "God-centered" approach affects reality, world views and Christian ministry and practice.

A human-centered view of life is unstable. From what racial or cultural background do those at the center stem and what are their inclinations and desires? Why them and not me (or why me and not someone else)? Others would say, the point is not *which* person we are talking about at the center, but that the best way to encourage the multitude of individuals that comprise our world is to develop responsibility and act in a way coherent with others, to encourage each to see their value and importance. The view is that we need high self-esteem to engender responsibility and value and thereby create a non-selfish life. Consider who you are, what you have to offer, how important you are, love yourself – and then you'll be able to help others, have appropriate boundaries, and so on.

The trouble with the philosophy of self-esteem even in its most benign form is that it is also highly unstable. Can I really "esteem" myself? Certainly not as a Christian. The Bible makes it clear there is not a whole lot to esteem about myself. I am a sinner and should not esteem that. And even if we take things back to a "pre-fall" state, my esteem, my image, is not a "self-image" but a God image. There we have our first clue of what a God-centered approach to life does. By contrast, it is unstable, even in the Garden of Eden, to develop a view of life that depends upon self-esteem. In fact, we may wonder whether that very desire is not itself the essence of sin.

The Bible never intends Christians to focus upon "self-esteem." When we think of ourselves, and what is good about us, all of it goes back to God and the redeeming work of Christ; it is "by the grace of God" that we are what we are. Human-centeredness, of whatever kind, seems inherently unstable (not to mention unbiblical, selfish and sinful). Even the laudable intended effects of "self-esteem" are based upon a foundation that cannot sustain such weight.

But, someone might say, is not the whole of modern moral philosophy and political economy based upon the "individual"? Is this not what capitalism is about? Are we suggesting some form of communitarianism, if not communism? Is not the very success of modern life built upon this idea of the freedom of the individual? And is this "individualism" not really a form of human-centeredness? What are we saying, then? Are we saying we want to get rid of this individualism and replace it with a theocracy? Or at least an over-arching religious framework? How can that work in practice in a modern secular state (very different from the Puritan eighteenth-century colony in which Edwards lived)?

These are good questions. Indeed, the modern concept of the individual appears to be derived from a humanistic sense of the freedom of individual rights. On the contrary, however, individual freedoms and self-expression can be guaranteed only by the assertion of God, and a God-centered view of life. There have been (and are) religious dictatorships. But there have also been (and are) atheistic dictatorships. The point is that, while we may rejoice in the separation of church and state, the freedom to take or leave God in any formal sense of religious expression, these very freedoms were won and found space to flourish within distinctly *Christian* philosophical frameworks. We believe in the freedom of individuals because the Bible teaches the sanctity of life. Humans are valuable because God has invested in them his image. In fact, these very cherished freedoms are most at threat from a human-centered view of life, because then there rapidly becomes no objective reason to value humans of whatever kind, as opposed to only the most useful humans, or the most productive humans. We should also mention the presence and effects of human-centeredness in the church. The greatest sign of the lack of a truly godly spirit and a worldly affection in any particular church is a lack of submission. We are intended to submit to one another and to submit to our leaders. But a human-centered view of life counters this with the feelings "What about me? Why should I take orders from anyone? I think I'm right. What makes someone else's opinion better than mine?" Very soon, all semblance of community is threatened by the ugly Medusa-like head of self in its many manifestations. Again, a God-centered view of life is the antidote. Paul tells us as much: "Submit to one another out of reverence for Christ" (Ephesians 5:21). It's all about Christ, not about me, him, her or even us, and therefore we express our most profound worship of Jesus in our mutual submission. If that is the effect of a human-centered approach applied in different forms to life, what are the effects of a God-centered approach to life?

THE RESULTS OF BEING GOD-CENTERED

Current scientific developments have given rise to the view that there is increasing hope for science to take on a more "religious" or Christian feel. There is the anthropic principle, the idea that the universe looks remarkably well fitted to have been designed for human survival. There are growing fractures within the neo-Darwinian framework, exploited by some and countered by others with "Intelligent Design Theory." There are new views of molecular chemical structures that appear to give new life to the idea that their mode of operation requires more than mere chance for them to have begun. In the realm of physics, biology or chemistry, then, some see hope for science to begin to function at least not along purely naturalistic or atheistic lines. Others feel this is reductionistic and devoid of real explanatory power: can there not be hope for a new "paradigm shift" to a better, more productive (and more Christian) mode of science's operations?

To tackle these issues here in any satisfying depth is impossible. But Edwards' God-centeredness does help. We do not need to look for a "gap" to feel comfortable about faith in God. What we need is to apply a view of God that sees all existence as constantly held up by God. Also, important as the scientific debates are, it is the sense, feeling, affection, heart that matter. And this heart needs to be imbued with a sense of God's presence – in the laboratory as much as the sanctuary.

In the realm of contemporary philosophy, the most promising area for Christians has been the developments within epistemology, the discipline of how we know things. While the impossibility of rational and public (as opposed to private, traditional or emotional) faith in God has been long held to be "proven," recently some have turned the game on its head, and (as in the famous description of the theologian Karl Barth's effect on the liberal scholarship of his day) set off a bomb in the secularist playground. How does Edwards' God-centeredness help here?

Well, Edwards would not be happy merely to record God as the foundation, as some recent Christian philosophers have asserted. Nor would he have been content to create a situation whereby faith in God was considered merely a legitimate option. These are huge gains. But Edwards wanted an epistemology of God not just as the foundation but as the pinnacle, the middle and the whole superstructure as well. By this means, he wanted to create not so much a formal academic reply to modernistic ways of framing how we know things, but a sensitivity to knowledge that allows us to realize that it is all from God, for God, and out of God's "mind." He simplified the issues by describing reality in a far less materialistic way than we are familiar with.

What this really means is that we are able to talk about God as rational (Edwards described how he felt that even the Trinity could be proved on the basis of pure reason), we may describe "evidences" for the resurrection or the historical reliability of the Bible (Edwards did that kind of thing at great length in his *History of the Work of Redemption*), but *none* of this is done *in the same way* or *on the same terms* as a philosophy of knowledge that jarringly claims that any amount of knowledge of God must be insufficient knowledge by definition. In Edwards' mindset almost the reverse was true: his view of life and knowledge was so radically God-centered that our very existence, our actual *knowing* (not just the formal debates about structure but our current mental processes) are expressive of the immediate creative power of God.

This leads to a different, and in essence more Christian, view of God, life and knowledge. How would Edwards' God-centeredness fare in discussion with our various current ethical questions and challenges? What impact does this view of life have upon questions of genetic cloning, stem-cell research, just wars, euthanasia, whether it is ever right to lie, or any other of the myriad questions that more classically define moral philosophy?

Again Edwards' God-centeredness gives not so much an answer to these questions as hints and suggestions of a different way of approaching them. Is it right to lie to the Nazi who asks whether you are sheltering Jews? Edwards has no answer to that question, for historical anachronistic reasons. The same is true for genetic challenges, and the problems posed by modern techniques of warfare. Nonetheless, Edwards' God-centeredness provides a view of life as so under God's hand that any amount of disobedience to his law, however small, however slight, offends him. It puts the fear of God back into ethical questions.

All of these questions stumble, of course, because in essence they weigh up the rights and wrongs on the basis of what will be most good for the greatest number of people. But what if "human-centeredness" was not the issue at all? What if the only question that mattered was what glorified God? Is there really any doubt about what he thinks about this? Is not the issue really whether we are willing to stand up for God, despite our apparently losing out? If we say we believe in him but do not do what he says (see the book of James), are we Christians at all?

This placing God back in the center changes the whole perspective. How about the much-vexed issues of politics and globalization?

Again, Edwards certainly never considered politics in a modern media-driven society, or an economy as interwoven globally as most economies are today.

How, though, would Edwards' approach speak to these bastions of the capitalist way? What would be his response to a G8 Summit or a World Bank directors' meeting? It would be nothing other than to put God back at the center. Instead of being driven by questions of the market, he would want to be driven by a concern for God and his glory. This does not make market considerations unimportant, or not present, or even not controlling the agenda of such meetings. But the whole tenor, the approach, the intention, the aim, the goal, the motivation, the heart, the consideration, would not be "What can I get out of this? What can my country get out of this?" Or even "What can the global community get out of this?" It would simply be "What will please God in this?"

6.

SECONDARY ISSUES SOMETIMES HAVE PRIMARY IMPORTANCE

Long has my memory recorded one brief encounter with a certain church strategist. We were talking about innovative ways to reach out to the emerging culture with the biblical gospel of Jesus. "You have to remember," he said to me as we parted, "you're in sales." This chapter is my journey of discovery with Edwards as guide to a realization that the gospel is a story to be told, not a product to be sold.

WHAT EVERYONE THINKS THEY KNOW ABOUT EDWARDS

There are two pieces of information everyone knows about Jonathan Edwards. One is that he preached a sermon called "Sinners in the Hands of an Angry God." I trust I have already contextualized that sermon, so we realize that, while Edwards certainly preached and believed in hell, the subject of eternal damnation was not a tool of theological terrorism. Edwards preached hell as a compassionate proclamation of a truth that, he felt, must be heard and understood as a priority. Most opponents of hellfire preaching are really against it because they don't believe in the existence of hell. People do not mind being warned of something if they think the danger is real.

Edwards believed in hell and therefore warned us of its awful reality. That sermon is also contextualized by Edwards' voluminous sermons on other biblical subjects, including Christ's love and our love for one another, as well as his books and notes on a wide range of theological and practical matters. The other piece of information almost everyone knows about Edwards is that he was thrown out of his church. This is somewhat surprising, but fact, as they say, is stranger than fiction. Edwards, the leader of several internationally famous "awakenings," was an extremely successful pastor and was at the core of that revival known as the "Great Awakening." Edwards was a well-known Christian leader, firmly established in his church, and therefore the idea of his suddenly losing his pastorate is extraordinary.

Perhaps the most moving of Edwards' sermons is his "Farewell Sermon." While alluding to the difficulties that had briefly and with unexpected violence encapsulated his ministry at Northampton, he emphasizes the providence of God and the eternal bond that unites pastor and people. I suspect not a dry eye in the house.

Different theories have developed to explain Edwards' strange ejection. One of the most popular interpretations is that Edwards came up against powerful factions in the town of Northampton. Before his removal from the pulpit, his greatest supporter and friend, also one of the most powerful people in the region, had died. Without him, this theory says, Edwards rapidly became exposed politically. It is certainly plain that in Northampton there had long been divisions between one family and another, between this group and that, between the rich and the poor. Some of Edwards' earlier sermons explicitly addressed this problem. So this theory says Edwards was caught in the crossfire of a political dispute. Another interpretation is that Edwards was thrown out of his pastorate because he came to stand for a more authoritative, more hierarchical, more traditional way of society. There are records that hint at criticisms of Sarah Edwards' expensive wardrobe. Edwards wore an aristocratic wig, and one of the children of the more influential families when rebuked by Edwards said he would not give respect to "a wig." The times were changing, this interpretation goes; the culture was

rapidly moving from being agrarian to mercantile, from being hierarchical to democratic, from being a colony to being a republic. Class
clash, this theory asserts, was the reason for Edwards' ejection from
his pulpit: he was out of touch with the new more democratic forces at
play in contemporary society.

Yet another series of interpretations tends to avoid, or downplay,
most human and historical interpretations, and instead look at the
whole event purely as divine providence. Christians, of course, believe
that all events in our lives are under the providential guidance of
God. This event that Edwards and his family experienced can be no
exception. But Edwards' ejection from his pulpit in particular, some
would say, appears to be a remarkable providence, because in the com-
parative backwater of Stockbridge, where Edwards next went to carry
on a ministry to Native Americans and settlers on the frontier, he was
able to write many of his most famous books. Previously he did not
have the time to write such weighty tomes, but now he could put pen to
paper and churn out such classics as *The Freedom of the Will* and *The
End for Which God Created the World*. This theory, then, emphasizes
the providential.

We have only begun to touch on the range of possible interpretations that have been advanced. Others have intimated that Edwards'
ministry became just too intense after a while, almost as if the people
needed a break. But I wish to suggest that Edwards' removal from the
pastorate was for exactly the reasons it appeared to be.

It was called the "Communion Controversy," and the trouble with
many analysts is that they find it hard to believe a controversy about
communion could really be what would cause Edwards to get thrown
out of his job. It just seems too minor a matter. Too theoretical a
subject. Too lacking in bite to be the real issue. It must be, many seem
to feel, only the surface or apparent reason, with underneath another
reason for which communion came to be the excuse. Like children in
a playground fighting over a football, where the real conflict is about
who is in control of the playground and the school, so the people of

Northampton could not actually have been fighting about communion, but about power, control, money or class.

I believe, however, the controversy was precisely about communion. That was the real issue. This all comes back to the title of this chapter: "Secondary issues sometimes have primary importance." Yes, communion appears to be a secondary issue, but actually here, Edwards believed, it was something of fundamental importance. He was not arguing, as in the Middle Ages, over how many angels can fit on the head of a pin, but, he believed, over the very nature of the church, salvation and the matter of the gospel itself. Obviously we do not want to say that secondary issues always have primary importance; otherwise there would be no secondary issues. But in this instance, for various reasons, Edwards became convinced that communion was of primary importance.

THE COMMUNION CONTROVERSY

The journey was not easy for Edwards. For a long time he agreed with, or accepted, the church structure his grandfather had instituted at Northampton and throughout the Connecticut River Valley. It was only later in his ministry, upon reflection, that he began to realize the real issues at stake and the problems it had caused. Edwards began to understand that this "half-way covenant," far from salvaging the nature of the church and the matter of salvation in Puritan New England, was thoroughly undermining both. New England Puritans were Congregationalists and therefore had a high view of church membership. The members of the church were involved in church government; they voted on a variety of matters (like who was going to be their pastor – or, in Edwards' case after the debacle, who was *not* going to be their pastor). When the Puritans arrived in New England, they came with a full deck of cards of converts, as it were. You did not make that journey, dangerous and perilous, from England to New England unless you believed you were a true born-again Christian. The next generation, of course, were brought up in the faith and trained carefully in Christian doctrine. Everyone knew the message of Christ and could recite the catechism. But not everyone had really experienced grace.

We can begin to imagine the scene. The church was completely dominant in the social setting. It was the centerpiece of the town. Being a member of the church was of great social, as well as spiritual, importance. The children of the settlers were duly, according to Congregationalist doctrine, baptized as infants. They then grew up learning the catechism and came to the stage when they were to take communion and become full members of the church. Some of them, however, had not, knew they had not and would make no profession of having experienced grace. In Edwards' phrase, they had no sense of divine things. They had not been born again. They knew it. Yet they wanted to be part of the church, for they understood its social and political importance in society.

What to do? Should they be denied entry to the church because they were not real Christians but only nominal Christians? But how could they be refused the rights of communion when they had been baptized as infants?

Solomon Stoddard, Edwards' grandfather, came up with a novel solution. He taught that communion was not just a meal for the converted, the Christian meal of celebration of what Jesus had done on the cross, but was also a "Converting Ordinance." That meant that not only was it *all right* for nominal Christians, professedly not saved, to take communion; it was actually a *good thing* for them to do so, and wrong to refuse them access to communion, for communion could help them become saved.

This was the situation Edwards inherited from his grandfather. Many full members of the church would attend religiously every Sunday and partake in church meetings, and were respected citizens, but had not made a profession of personal faith in Jesus.

This legacy created the Communion Controversy. Edwards slowly saw what a terrible mistake Stoddard had made. He tried to turn back to the original Puritan way of insisting that full membership of the church required not just a profession of faith in Jesus in the sense of saying, "Yes, I believe Jesus existed, died and rose again," but a profession of faith in Jesus in the sense of "I personally believe in Jesus, have trusted him for my salvation and have experienced the saving grace of God." This testimony of experience is what Edwards wanted.

It takes just a little imagination, or a bit of experience of church communities, to realize the kinds of problem this immediately caused. The church was packed with people who had access to all the privileges of membership – including voting and taking communion – but who had not been converted. Now Edwards was saying this was wrong. They should not receive communion or be members. It was easy in this context for Edwards to be caricatured as authoritarian, traditionalist, out of touch, high-handed, by the people he opposed or who opposed him.

The real issue, though, remained communion. Because of the theological and historical momentum that led to the Communion Controversy, the debate was not about "Where exactly should this resistance chalice be placed?" or "Should we use grape juice or wine?" or even, more substantively, "What is the right biblical way to understand how communion functions to encourage and edify the believer?" The debate was about the nature of the church. Is the church a collection of all the citizens of a town who unite to go through a ceremony, or a congregation of the faithful, those who have truly experienced grace? Ironically for the New England Puritans the historical development of their churches rapidly moved in the direction of establishing a church for all rather than only for those who were saved. Edwards stood against this historical stream. He said, 'No, communion is not a converting ordinance; it is only for those who have been converted.' As such, the debate was not only about the nature of the church; it was also about the nature of the gospel. What converts people? Is it religious ceremony or communion? Or are people converted by the proclamation of the good news of Jesus through the Word of truth, the Scriptures?

So, I believe, the reason that Edwards was ejected from his pulpit was the Communion Controversy. As always when trying to understand a figure from the past, we have to make the imaginative leap to under-stand the real issue rather than assuming it.

HOW DIFFERENT ARE WE?

This is worlds as well as centuries away from contemporary attitudes to Christianity. Influenced by the reaction of the 1960s and 1970s against institutions of any kind, and the church in particular, contemporary attitudes to Christianity are thoroughly non-ecclesiastical. People generally do not just have a "low-church" view; they have a "low view of the church." The two are not the same, though. When, as has happened since the sixties or so, seekers and outsiders to Christianity have said they 'like Jesus but can't stand the church', this has generated a new approach to church whereby the role, value and doctrine of the church has been greatly underemphasized.

We, in conservative Christian circles, have vigorously maintained the *message* of the gospel but, at least in some areas and among some movements, have begun to lose any profound grasp of the community of Christ. We have rightly said that a relationship with God is a personal matter. In our context, though, it has become but a step, and a step many of us have unthinkingly taken, to acquiesce that a relationship with God is a purely *individual* matter. This is practical heterodoxy. Jesus said you can identify his disciples by the kind of relationship they have with *one another,* by the "love" they have for one another.

According to Jesus, the key sign of a strong and true personal rela-tionship with God is our communal interaction with each other. Jesus rarely uses the word "church," but he teaches Christian community everywhere. He who has been forgiven by God, Jesus says, must forgive others. This is so strongly emphasized that the Lord's Prayer places linguistic priority on its head to underline the point: "For if you forgive men when they sin against you, your heavenly Father will also forgive you" (Matthew 6:14). Jesus is not teaching that our forgiveness is rewarded with God's forgiveness, but that an essential sign of our forgiveness is living in a forgiven community of relationships with other people.

So while our underemphasis upon church is understandable, and occasionally a useful apologetic move (we do not preach the church; we preach Christ), our modern attitudes to church have become profoundly influenced by the world's attitude to community. This means that community becomes mercantile, something we can buy into or out of. There is no commitment in community; but without commitment, community just becomes a unit – a single person in isolation, touching other lives but never integrating with them.

The easiest way to appreciate the profound lack of the communal emphasis in modern churches is to pay a visit to non-Western Bible-believing churches. Go to Africa, Asia or the republics of the former Soviet Union and you will find that their churches do not act like polarized individuals clubbed together, but like a body, where each member is a part of the other and belongs to the other.

As L. P. Hartley once wrote, "the past is a foreign country," and when we look at Edwards' embroilment in the Communion Controversy, we see just the tip of an iceberg of a totally different attitude to being church. What was done in church, what was thought about church, how the church acted, mattered to Edwards in a way it does not matter to us. We tend to run the church in a programmatic fashion, because we view it in a pragmatic way. We have personal interactions with friends in the church, of course, but the church itself we view as a marketed institution with no meaningful personal interactions, but only programs to offer. All our attitudes to what we often dismiss summarily as "secondary issues" about the church would be transformed if we took on an approach that was more corporeal, intimate, personal, Edwardean and biblical.

Much would change. It would matter what we think about baptism, communion, church leadership and government. It would matter how we structure our churches, how we treat each other. It would not matter as much as the gospel of Jesus Christ, but the church is still an expression of that gospel, bears witness to that gospel and has modes of operation described and taught in the pages of the New Testament. So the key difference between now and then is not just that Edwards was a Puritan, who like all good Puritans believed the New Testament taught us not merely the gospel, but also how to do church. The key difference is also that Edwards' attitude to the Communion Controversy witnessed to a higher view of the church, its role, significance, relationships and actions, not a "high-church" view, a higher view, therefore, that surely must be biblical. Is this not 'the church of the living God, the pillar and foundation of the truth' (1 Timothy 3:15)?

WHAT WOULD AN EDWARDS-LIKE ATTITUDE LOOK LIKE TODAY?

What does this mean in practice? Should we not have fellowship with people with a slightly different view of communion from us? Surely one of the great problems with the Protestant church in general is its tendency to spin off into factions and become sectarian? Should we not make every effort, as Paul also enjoins us to do, to keep the unity of the Spirit through the bond of peace (Ephesians 4:3)?

Again the point, to my mind, is not *what* Edwards believed about communion (though that was not a nit-picky minor matter either), but that he believed church practice was so important. Or, to put it another way, *what* Edwards believed about communion was evidence of his more basic, foundational commitment to issues of first importance, like the gospel and the nature of the church. For Edwards, to state clearly and practice faithfully that only the genuinely converted could partake of communion was a message about the reality of conversion and the nature of the church. The church, Edwards felt, was a communion of saints, not a representation of the local citizens of the town. As such, communion itself must witness to this reality. Communion could not be a "converting ordinance," as his grandfather had thought.

In fact, because our culture does not consider doctrinal questions of great importance, it is *frequently* only when we find a matter with which our culture strongly disagrees that we find out where our basic allegiance lies. The issue itself may not (from a gospel point of view) be terribly important. But if our culture says one thing and the Bible says another, then which of these two voices we listen to and obey evidences our basic loyalty. There are many issues like this today. Most of them are controversial because they are by the nature of the question matters about which our culture feels strongly and around which the Bible speaks differently.

Take the issue of homosexuality. It is true the Bible does not say much about homosexuality. It is also true Jesus never said anything at all about homosexuality specifically, though his attitude to marriage and sexuality were entirely heterosexual. To say, though, that the Bible does not address the matter of homosexuality is simply false. It does – in both the Old and the New Testament. Now in our culture, increasingly, homosexuality, homosexual marriage, and all the cluster of social issues that surround these have become issues that raise the flag of social freedom.

It is a civil right, some feel, to practice sexually however we feel, and it is a civil right for the state formally (and thus publicly in marriage) to countenance such behavior of whatever kind. Of course no-one takes these arguments to their logical extreme: What if I want to have four wives? Why shouldn't the state allow this? But nonetheless the point is powerfully made these days in our culture that homosexual orientation is a fact of nature, that homosexual practice is a civil right, and therefore that homosexual marriage is a freedom in which all who wish it should be allowed to participate.

What is the church's response? Well, the first question of course is, 'What does the Bible say?' More extensive surveys of the matter have been done elsewhere and now is not the time to analyze all the pertinent texts (yet again) in great detail. Suffice it to say that in my (and many others') opinion the Bible speaks clearly against homosexual practice. What, then, should the church say about this? It should speak against homosexual practice, while, of course, loving and reaching out to the homosexually orientated with the gospel of Jesus Christ.

But the waters are often muddied *precisely because* this is such a controversial issue. That it is so controversial, however, tells us where our loyalty lies with regard to Scripture, Christ and God. If the Bible speaks clearly about this matter, if our culture speaks the opposite, what I think about homosexuality (if I am not ignorant of what the Bible says) will reveal my view of the Bible and Christ. Homosexuality and our opinions about it are not salvation issues, but they may, in our context, witness (as little else can, given our doctrinal vagueness) where our heart is, what we really believe about God, and under whose authority we exist, that of God or that of the World.

There are many other ways of performing the same diagnostic test. I am not saying my opinion about homosexuality, women's ministry, baptism, communion, or anything else like that, is itself a matter of salvation. I am saying that at certain cultural moments, or in certain situations, which side I come down on may be an extremely pertinent and accurate sign as to whether I have really been saved.

Take another example, less culturally controversial but in some ways more divisive among conservative evangelicals. I am a Baptist. That does not mean I was brought up a Baptist (I was brought up in the Church of England). Nor does it mean I have certain social tastes or patterns of traditional behavior that are Baptist (though I may or may not). All it means is that I believe the New Testament teaches believers' baptism. Not everyone does. There are wiser Bible teachers than me who are paedobaptists (they believe in infant baptism). However, I also know of many who are really Baptists but who work within paedo-baptist churches because baptism is a "secondary issue," and they feel the paedobaptist churches are more "strategic" for the gospel. This is a mistake. Even if baptism is only a matter of conscience, it must be wrong to act against your conscience.

Or let us ask this question: "How do I know whether I am *truly* following Christ in a culture where there is little suffering for Christ?" Of course I should not go out and seek suffering. But when there is an issue where going one way follows the biblical material (even if only according to my conscience) and where going the other does not follow the biblical material, but is easier and more prestigious, then where is my heart? Is it in Christ? Or is it in finding an easy, well-paid job, career or place in the social stratum of my culture? Of course those series of questions could in some instances be asked the other way around, in a different social context. Nonetheless, they remain as important identifications of where I am with Jesus.

AGAINST DUMBED-DOWN CHURCH

Such careful discernment flies in the face of our dumbed-down religion, where doctrine is rarely considered important, where comfort and security trump sacrifice and commitment. It runs against the stream, which is exactly what Christian discipleship always does. It is either the narrow way, the hard road, or the broad, easy way that leads to destruction. There must be some rub, some friction, with our commitments determining our direction, or we are just pulled hither and thither by religious fashion or cultural hegemony.

Doctrinal distinctions can solve the cynicism that is so often the by-product of faddish approaches to the church. When the church acts poorly, it always produces people whose personal relationship with God becomes threatened. We associate God with his church. The solution to cynicism about the church is not to downplay, ignore or move out of the church, but to redeem the church, purify, reform and change it to be more in line with biblical ideals. When people treat Jesus as the chief executive officer of a marketing organization, the church rapidly disintegrates into a system in which people are treated like products, salvation like deals, and where the bottom line is the budget, not the glory of God.

Many churches have bought attitude into the idea that what matters is numbers, the amount of money or the attendance on Sunday. The numbers game is a great temptation because it hides a real truth. Yes, getting more people "saved" matters; getting more people into heaven is of the greatest importance. Yet simply getting more bums on seats is not the same as getting more worshipers in Spirit and in truth. If we turn our church venture into a marketing copy of the way a large company is organized, we may momentarily get more people into the church. But the "church" may have lost its distinction of being a true church of God. It could have become nothing more than a vaguely religious gathering, or a society built around basic moral axioms, a gathering where people float like amoebas in a soup of doctrinal spinelessness.

The gospel of Jesus Christ is not a product to be marketed: it is a message to be proclaimed. Surely we understand this from the Bible? The gospel of Jesus Christ must influence and challenge *how* we do church and not just be a hook to reach out to more fish. The gospel needs to have a reforming power over our ecclesiastical institutions. This certainly is the great challenge in the Western churches. The need for change – gospel change. Edwards did not appeal for traditional ways of doing church as opposed to the modern. He supported the innovative field preacher George Whitefield. In many ways, churches should always be modernizing. The church is a dynamic institution that needs constantly to be changed, purified and developed to be more like Christ. Even the old Puritan catechism says the church is not perfect, but is being perfected. Churches need to change to meet the different strategic challenges of each new era. The question is not, therefore, whether we think the church "should move with the times" or not.

Of course the church *should* move with the times (in some ways) and should *not* move with the times (in other ways). The church should not move with the trends in culture with regard to sexual morality or greed or any of the other common, growing patterns of moral depravity so widespread in our times. But the church *should* move with the times when it comes to, for example, using modern sound equipment, or microphones, projectors, screens, computers, email, the Internet and so on. In fact the church has often been at the forefront of these changes, or made exponential use of them, with regard, for instance, to the printing presses and the great success of the Gutenberg Bible. What, then, does all this mean in the most practical and down-to-earth way? It means, on occasions, depending on the situation and its significance within the culture, being willing to insist on purity and the best standard of practice with regard to certain only secondary or relatively unimportant issues. This is not moralism or legalism – it is biblical faithfulness.

7.

EFFECTIVE LEADERSHIP MUST BE BIBLICALLY INTELLIGENT LEADERSHIP

On the RMS *Titanic* all is calm, not a cloud in sight. Indeed, the atmosphere is beyond pleasant, with a soft band playing, culinary delights on offer and a social cast of luminaries with whom to converse. But disaster, in the form of a largely hidden iceberg, is about to strike. Books have been written and a blockbuster film made about what caused the captain of the *Titanic* unwittingly to lead so many to their death.

One could not fault the decorated helmsmen at its rudder, or the construction of the ship, but in all the hullabaloo somewhere along the line the most fundamental purpose of the seafaring ship was lost: to get people safely from point A to point B. I doubt many of us feel the *Titanic* would have been safer for having a lecture hall's worth of academics on its deck, but a person in charge at the crucial moment whose mind was clear about the most important issues might well have saved the day. Who can say?

Perhaps the most dangerous missing component aboard the ship *Evangelicalism,* with its "unsinkable" confidence, is the surrender of the wheel to unthinking leaders.

THE PLACE OF THE MIND

The mind has played an ambiguous part in Christian history. Jesus, as far as we know, was not formally educated but learnt his trade as a carpenter. Paul, on the other hand, was a "Pharisee of Pharisees," top of the class of an elite band of theological intelligentsia. The early Christian heresy Gnosticism emphasized a secret "knowledge" that was the private property of the initiated few. It also tended towards a philosophy whereby the body was bad and the mind, the *gnōsis,* "knowledge," good. Such an elitist tendency to give advantage to the high IQ was never intended by Scripture, where we find that even Paul can tell us to worship God with the sacrifice of "our bodies" as much as our minds.

Moving on further through history we find a common struggle to find appropriate balance on this matter. The rediscovery of pagan philosopher Aristotle's writings led to a crisis of faith for some in medieval Christendom, until Thomas Aquinas managed to formulate an expression of Christianity coordinate with Aristotle. Who domesticated whom is still debated. And then today some tell us, in effect, to throw away our minds in order to "just believe," building probably unknowingly on the existentialist philosophy which put that catchphrase "leap of faith" in a wrong context. Yet, at the other extreme are those who give the impression that without a working definition of alien righteousness, prelapsarianism and over-realized eschatology to hand, the pearly gates themselves may stay stubbornly closed to our timid, under-educated appearance.

Given that Balaam's donkey was used to convey God's message, we might go so far as to say that, biblically speaking, it is quite clear that intelligence is not necessary for usefulness in the Lord's service. However, taking that parabolic narrative to an extreme, we might also conclude from the donkey's unfortunate rebuke of Balaam that humanity itself was no prerequisite for being used by God. Of course we would be right to conclude God is such that he can use the rolling spheres in the heavens to dance to his tune, the might of the Assyrian army to be his servant, as much as any more dignified *Homo sapiens*.

But such reflections seem to get us no nearer a solution to the age-old question 'How can I be most used by God?' Nor do they establish in what way intelligence, the mind and intellectual achievements are useful in the Christian cause or in Christian leadership.

A more fruitful approach would be to study the famous eleventh chapter of the book of Hebrews. There we find the author of Hebrews teaching us that the one point all the great heroes of the Old Testament had in common was not a natural faculty, but a spiritual attitude: faith. Here we find a key to the solution to our dilemma. Yes, God *can* use whomever and whatever he wants – but he *chooses* to use people of faith.

In other words, our intelligence, our natural capacities, be they large or small, are made useful to God by being directed by a principle of faith. The kind of person, the kind of leader, most effective in God's kingdom is, then, a *biblically* intelligent leader. That does not mean that his exam scores were especially high; it means simply that his whole being, mind and body are put to service at the feet of the Master.

THE EXAMPLE OF EDWARDS

Edwards epitomized this in an extreme way. His brain-processing speed was unusually fast and his mental "hard drive" unusually large. Nonetheless, what marked Edwards' thinking apart from his contemporaries' was not simply that he was more intelligent. It was the *kind* of intelligence Edwards employed, a biblically intelligent leadership. His blood, as Charles Spurgeon famously stated, ran "Bibline."

One contemporary of Edwards noticed that he studied the Bible more than any other pastor of his age. Edwards had a prodigious mental output. He has left behind not scores but thousands of pages of notes used to sharpen his mental skills. More remarkable still is the kind of notes these were: they began from the premise and promise of

Scripture. When I describe this approach of Edwards I say it was one of "reasoning after Scripture."

He did not let the authority of Scripture become a prison to his mind. Instead, God's Word rippled throughout Edwards' mind. Edwards had four implicit foundational principles that shaped his "biblical intelligence."

Principle 1: reason befriends faith

According to Edwards, unusually enough, the nature of the Trinity and our need for God's love were both accessible to pure reason. The Christian doctrine of the Trinity is normally understood to be a subject revealed in Scripture, not nature, but Edwards argued that *enlightened* rational deductions from principles in the Bible could prove the credibility of the Trinity. He speculated that the trinitarian essence of the Godhead was "within the reach of naked reason." He also considered humanity's need for the love of God "evident from mere reason" (T. A. Schafer [ed.], *The Works of Jonathan Edwards* [Yale University Press, 1994], vol. 13, p. 336).

Edwards even began to formulate these radical reflections into a proposed (though never completed) "Rational Account of Christianity." Some have suggested that this rationalism shows Edwards' deistic intoxication with the new science of the Enlightenment. Others believe that Edwards later grew out of his naive faith in reason. The truth is that Edwards never lost his rationality, nor supplanted his faith with it. Why? He believed that *in principle* reason is a friend of faith. Edwards explained the rationale for this principle: As "there may be deductions of reason from what has been said [in the Scripture]," therefore he was "not afraid to say twenty things about the Trinity which the Scripture never said" (T. A. Schafer [ed.], *Works of Jonathan Edwards*, vol. 13, p. 257). Edwards is not saying that Christianity is founded upon reason; he is saying that Christianity is foundationally reasonable. We might shake our head at the Trinity "being within reach of naked reason," but the principle of (spiritually) enlightened rationality is appropriate and appealing.

This principle is not confined to his private notebooks and miscellanies. His publicly preached congregational sermons revealed the same range of concepts. For instance, when Edwards described his approach to assessing spiritual experiences, to the forefront was the concept that God has left some matters for us to deduce from Scripture and reason. The very heart of spiritual experience, a "Divine and Supernatural Light," which is "immediately imparted to the soul by the Spirit of God," can be shown to be "both a Scriptural and Rational Doctrine" (E. Hickman [ed.], *The Works of Jonathan Edwards* [Banner of Truth], 1988, vol. 2, p. 12).

Today we tend to distrust our reasoning. We are more likely to make judgments based on our gut than our mind. We want to "go with our instincts." We don't rely upon a carefully considered appreciation of all the salient details, logically analyzed, weighed and considered, and finally decided. We rely upon our feelings. Certainly when it comes to getting a mortgage, doing our tax returns or completing an algebra test, we engage our logical and rational faculties. With God, however, we assume the game is different; we somehow feel that rationality, especially science, is inimical to healthy faith. Edwards wants to persuade us that the converse is true. In fact, reason befriends faith. They are not contrasting, or conflicting, informational sources, but collaborative ventures. Comparing reason with faith is not comparing apples with oranges; it is not a category error to discuss the two in the same breath. A healthy faith is a reasonable faith and a healthy reason is faithful.

Because Edwards was not frightened of his mind, or of the conclusions that exercising his mental capacities would create, he was enabled to engage with contemporary ideas with fervor, verve and considerable panache. If we foundationally, as a principle, view faith as an enemy of reason we will be driven, in the modern world, to two possible modes of living. Either we will be in an escapist, private world ignorant of and inimical to the discoveries of science. Or we will abandon our faith, hopelessly persuaded of the victory of science. If, on the other hand, as a foundational principle we are persuaded that faith and reason can coexist, we will find ways to critique some so-called certainties of science and develop creatively faithful responses to modern issues. What makes Edwards such an awesome discussion partner is his unwavering commitment to orthodox faith and his unnervingly creative rational contributions. It all comes from this "biblical intelligence" and the principles on which it was based.

Principle 2: reason defends faith

Edwards believed reason and evidence were essential elements of a vigorous defense of the truthfulness of Christianity. Some, however, disagree. Charles Spurgeon famously quipped once, "Defend the Bible? I'd rather defend a lion." The Bible, he was saying, can look after itself. It has teeth. It is sharper than a double-edged sword. With this certain confidence in the spiritual power of the Bible and the preached word, Edwards would have no qualms. The apparent divergence between Spurgeon's remark and Edwards is a matter of tone and style, not of substance.

Others disagree, however, on the basis of more essential philosophical differences. They would argue that if my faith in God is based upon a logical or historical deduction, it is then based upon a human matter and not therefore ultimately grounded upon God himself. Someone, they would say, may be persuaded of the truthfulness of Christianity on the basis of reason or evidence, but the "faith" thus generated is not the pure faith of unadulterated trust in God, despite the whisperings of the world.

Edwards believed this non-evidential or non-rational approach to establishing the truthfulness of Christianity served only to show, in the mind of the skeptic, that Christianity was not really reasonable at all. So he strongly opposed the unnamed author of "Christianity not founded on argument," who said that arguing for the truths of natural religion had "done more harm than good." To Edwards this made Christianity seem unreasonable by denying the reliability of reason (no. 1297, the "Miscellanies").

In fact Edwards listed many proofs for the historicity of the Bible in his notebooks. Numbers 131, 202, 276, 382 and 465 of the "Miscellanies" all take up this theme of giving proofs for the reliability of the Bible. Edwards' "Notes on the Scriptures" have a similar emphasis in numbers 220, 222 and 445. But that numerical list by no means exhausts Edwards' commitment to arguing for the rational and evidential truthfulness of Christianity. He made a historical ethical judgment to support the Old Testament faith against pagan religions. The rite of circumcision selected the "Jewish Religion" as of "divine authority," because it contradicted human pride and lust while "False religions always spare those two lusts of lasciviousness and pride" (T. A. Schafer [ed.], *Works of Jonathan Edwards*, vol. 13, p. 394). He also defended the historicity of the Old Testament. Edwards aimed to show that the Pentateuch was historical by "Evidences There are that the Facts of the MOSAIC HISTORY never could be forged" ("Subjects of Inquiry," p. 14; unpublished note). He resolved apparent historical difficulties in the text of the Old Testament books, arguing, for instance, that the "Great difficulty" that Ahaziah seemed to be two years older than his father in 2 Chronicles 22:1–4 is resolved by arguing that the number refers not to Ahaziah's age but to the age of his household, thereby including the years of his father to match the total recorded (S. J. Stein [ed.], *Works of Jonathan Edwards*, [Yale University Press, 1998], vol. 15, pp. 158–160).

In the New Testament the approach is the same. The Gospels are "the Facts of the X[Chris]tian Religion" ("Rough Notes on the Truth of the Christian Religion"; unpublished note). With regard to the Acts and Epistles, Edwards reminds himself, "In reading the ACTS & the EPISTLES to observe the Evidences of the Fact of X "[Christ's] Resurrection & other Chief Facts Relating to X [Christ]" ('Subjects of Inquiry," p. 17; unpublished note).

Edwards pens a reconciliation of the Gospel accounts of the resurrection, though, despite the reference to the four evangelists in the note's title, it is only the Synoptic Gospels Edwards cites: "The accounts of the four Evangelists Concerning the Resurrection of Christ Reconciled" ("Notes on the Scriptures," p. 220). Finally, Edwards sees the historical resurrection event as the factual cornerstone of the Christian faith. He argues that Christ really died because he did not feign death or "swoon," (no. 152, the "Miscellanies"), that the resurrection was full proof of Christ's authority as "witches juggling is at an end when they are dead" (no. 313, the "Miscellanies"), that the Old Testament argued it as a proof of a prophet (no. 321a, the "Miscellanies") and that Christ's resurrection is the fact that separates Christianity from Islam (no. 1334, the "Miscellanies").

The principle behind this long series of evidences for the trustworthiness of Christianity is that reason defends faith. According to Edwards, the Bible has a real spatiotemporal location, meaning that it sets "forth things just as they happened" (no. 6, the "Miscellanies"). Not only is the Bible principally historical, so it is correct to give historical evidences for its truthfulness, but this very susceptibility to rationality is also part of the persuasiveness of Scripture. Therefore, the grand difference between Islam and Christianity is that, while Christianity was established by "Light, Instruction & Knowledge, Reason & Enquiry," "Mahometanism was propagated not by Light & Instruction but by darkness; not by Encouraging Reasoning and Search; but by discouraging Knowledge & learning" (no. 1334, the "Miscellanies"). The reasonableness of Christianity is what separates it from false revelations.

Principle 3: reason intends faith

Edwards' third implicit principle was that such a rational and evidential approach to defending the faith did not serve merely to give us a probable certainty of its truth. He did not think natural revelation proved God only *probably* existed. He believed our natural capacities and the natural components of the universe together established that God certainly existed.

In this respect, Edwards differed from the apologetic approach of Bishop Butler and his famous *Analogy of Religion, Natural and Revealed* (1736), so influential on later apologists. Butler believed there was an "analogy" between the revelation of God in nature and the revelation of

God in Scripture from which could be determined the probable truth of the Christian faith in God. Edwards, however, went further. In a sermon on Romans 1:20, he proposed such evidences for God do not give "meer probability" or "strong presumption" or even "much evidence," but rather "absolute certain & full infallible demonstration." Edwards was determined to impress on his hearers the ease and the "clearness of the evidence." He argued that "'Tis impossible for us to conceive how G[od] could have [given] Greater Evid[ence] of his being than he has done," for even 'if we would see millions of miracles wrought i.e. things out of any steady course of nature [we] could see no more in such works than in the works we see" (unpublished sermon).

Part of this is Edwards' view of God's immediate activity in the natural world. Some scholars have called it a doctrine of 'continuous creation'. Edwards felt that not only did God create the world, not only did he sustain it, but he continually recreated ("as it were" a classic Edwards nuance) the whole universe each moment. Some of this arose from a reflection upon the Authorized Version of Revelation 4:11: 'Thou art worthy, O Lord, to receive glory and honor and power: for thou has created all things, and for thy pleasure they are and were created' (av). With such a view of reality, it is impossible to conceive of more concrete evidences of God's existence than our existence and the continuing motion of the planets and molecules. It also, though (along with both the previous principles) depends on the final implicit principle of Edwards' "biblical intelligence."

Principle 4: faith mends reason

Edwards finally felt, though, that all this rationality was nonetheless insufficient. Two massive sermons (one already mentioned on Romans 1:20 and the other on Psalm 14:1) set out Edwards' pastoral approach to the matter. Yes, reason and science establish beyond question the truthfulness of Scripture. Yes, the Bible itself, by virtue of its author, is reasonable and therefore self-attests to its truthfulness. Yes, this is all true, yet many do not agree and still feel they are acting rationally and may themselves be clever people. How does Edwards square this circle? We must remember that Edwards was living at a time when skepticism was rampant, if politely disguised at times.

He does not go down the deist route of rejecting Scripture to rely upon rationality – or only that which common reason from nature suggests is true about God. Neither, though, does he reject reason to rely in a privatistic or quietistic way upon the special revelation of Scripture exclusive of rational verification. Instead, Edwards confirms that the reasonableness of Scripture is certain, indeed self-evident, yet many reject it, apparently for rational reasons, because their rationality, before conversion, does not function accurately. It is Edwards' doctrine of the fall that allows him to escape deism or privatized apologetics. He believes only a fully "enlightened" mind, one that has received the Holy Spirit, can see the truth that all these evidences point inexorably to God, but that a mind still in sin is in darkness.

This approach to apologetics was not unique to Edwards, though was perhaps most exhaustively developed by him. Charles Simeon, in Cambridge, England, developed a similar approach in that hothouse of the new learning. In "An Appeal to Men of Wisdom and Candour," preached before Cambridge University, Simeon argued that, to the "enlightened," revealed religion is reasonable: "though revealed religion is neither founded on human reason, nor makes its appeal to it; yet it is perfectly consistent with reason and approves itself to the judgment of everyone whose mind is enlightened by the Spirit of God," who have "enlightened reason" (H. D. McDonald, *Ideas of Revelation: An Historical Study,* 1700–1860 [London, 1959], p. 223).

Edwards' four principles of "biblical intelligence" – reason befriends faith, reason defends faith, reason intends faith and faith mends reason – had two implications for his practice of ministry.

Implications for practical ministry

First, Edwards' practical leadership style was profoundly influenced by these implicit principles. The effectiveness of his leadership was most evident at the time of the Great Awakening. With mass revival sweeping New England, there was great need for pastoral judgment. Some embraced not only the Great Awakening but also its radical fringe. These radicals came to accept "direct impressions" from God as of equal weight with Scripture. They boldly declared (on the basis of direct intuitions from God about who was and who was not converted) certain New England ministers to be not truly converted. The radicals even burnt books publicly as a testimony against all rational elements of faith. On the other hand, others totally rejected the Great Awakening as "enthusiasm." For the Puritans, "enthusiasm" was the term that reminded them of the woeful extremes of the radical Reformation. It was the claim that "God was within," not in the normal Christian sense of his presence by the Holy Spirit in regeneration, but in a mystical imbalanced claim to a hotline from God replacing the authoritative revelation of Scripture.

The Great Awakening was certainly a messy affair. It was not long before the international Evangelical Awakening, pioneered by George Whitefield and John Wesley, suffered disunity as its two luminaries disagreed over the relative merits of Calvinism and Arminianism. Whitefield and Wesley remained the best of friends, but they had more than their share of enemies in the established Church of England. When Whitefield came to town in New England, people would rush from miles around to hear him preach in the fields. The social upheaval of these events – in a society where the steepled Congregational Church on the green had dominated – was massive, and no doubt a precursor of the Industrial Revolution, the ending of the slave trade, and other social egalitarian movements.

So the threat to an establishment figure like Jonathan Edwards (the pastor of a prestigious pulpit) was clear. But Edwards embraced the Great Awakening. As mentioned in chapter 1, when George Whitefield preached at Northampton, Edwards wept throughout the sermon as he sat in the front pew. Edwards' wife, Sarah, marveled at the effect wrought on so many by the proclamation of the simplest truths of the gospel. Edwards had a big call to make regarding the Great Awakening and he got it just right, because he employed the principles of biblical intelligence.

Proverbs exalts wisdom beginning with the fear of the Lord. Edwards applied basic and traditional gospel teaching – that we can know the reality of a work of God by its fruits – to the Great Awakening. He observed some social chaos. He noticed changes of method and style. What he fixed his attention on, however, was the fruit of righteousness, joy, love and hope. This, he concluded, was and could only be the work of the Holy Spirit. He therefore taught into the situation, urging restraint where necessary and passionate enthusiasm elsewhere, and so became perhaps the most profound theologian of spiritual experience in the history of the Christian church.

Edwards' practice of pastoral ministry more generally was influenced by these same principles of biblical intelligence. Edwards viewed his pastoral vocation primarily as a gospel preacher and Bible teacher. In one sermon, delivered at the inauguration of another pastor, Edwards preached that a pastor should be a "burning and shining light." He used John the Baptist as the perfect example of a pastor pointing people to Jesus through the preached word. How would many of us characterize the roles and respon-sibilities of a pastor today? Would we not think more along the lines of a business model? Pastor as chief executive officer is a common, if unspoken, assumption today. But, according to Edwards, while he clearly believed in the authority of the pastor to lead his church, such leadership was given primarily through the teaching and preaching of the Word.

This was the standard job description of the pastor in those days. The Puritan model of pastor was not academic in the sense of the modern university professor. It was, however, a scholar-pastor, or (as Paul puts it in Ephesians 4:11) "pastor and teacher." The Puritans in general and Edwards in particular felt that the primary role of the pastor was to teach the Bible and preach the gospel. It is not hard to give biblical warrant to this view. Just a cursory glance at Ephesians 4 (the gift of "pastor-teacher" is joined in the Greek) or 1 Timothy 4 serves to confirm exactly this fundamental of the role of the pastor as primarily proclaiming God's Word.

IS THIS RELEVANT?

What is the relevance of Edwards' "biblical intelligence" today? Recent statistics continue to suggest that "unchurched" people are a growing phenomenon in the Western world, even in "Bible belt" areas, and especially in the old Christendom of Europe or the intellectual elite of, ironically enough, Edwards' own old revival stomping ground, New England. Why do many people in the West stop attending church? And what can be done about it?

Leaving aside the theological factors that are continually true (people do not go to church because they are sinners, God is sovereign over the growth of his church), the spiritual aspects pertinent today are readily observable. Why do people not go to church? Simply because they do not believe that the message of Christianity is true. This is what is normally behind all other reasons often expressed by the unchurched. They might say, "Why should I believe in God when I'm doing just fine?" Or even, "What's in it for me?"

But if someone is really persuaded that God is true, that sin is our condition, that heaven and hell are eternal realities, that Jesus is the only Savior, and that personal faith must be worked out in the family of a local fellowship, then these questions about the point of going to church are easily answered. "What's in it for me?" Salvation from eternal damnation, for one. "Why should I go when I'm doing just fine?" No, you're not doing just fine. Yet in our human folly we continue to churn out pastors primarily equipped to maintain the status quo, diminishing in numbers as our church attendance figures in the West are. We want managers. We even want marketers. Yet what we really need are *persuaders*. People who will, because of their professional background, personal qualities and persuasive abilities, be able to stand up and give credence to the age-old faith. Part of Edwards' appeal was simply that all who heard him knew he was remarkably bright. This certainly gave weight to his fervent warnings about hell. The subtext in many an Edwards sermon is, "If this man, who is so clever, believes these truths, which might seem so strange, should I not believe them too?"

Genius cannot be a prerequisite of Christian leadership, or the ranks of leaders would dwindle. We should not set the bar higher than Scripture does in respect of the qualifications for elders in our ministry. Yet part of the distinctive ability required is the ability to teach, and, today, that requirement is especially important. People need to know that the faith is understandable, real and believable. They need to be persuaded, not simply in a marketing catchphrase way that might gather more from the ranks of the already persuaded, but in a genuine, content-full and instructive manner that conveys information about the gospel in a compelling way.

For instance, Edwards formulated a series of theological questions, which he used as starting points for intense theological education of budding ministers. They are really quite demanding. There are questions about the truthfulness of the Trinity, questions that tackle the sinfulness of sin, questions about any number of matters from both a theological and an apologetic standpoint.

Obviously, the pastor of a church needs to engage in "pastoral" work, which in our current meaning tends to emphasize personal encounter and relationship-building, as well as managing the inevitable politics of the church. It may also be true that this side of pastoring was Edwards' weak link. Nonetheless, our tendency today is to neglect not the visitation, nor the management, nor the counseling, but the need for people who can be "burning and shining lights," who are able effectively and credibly to communicate the gospel in an increasingly post-Christian era. The world will look on in mockery if all our Christian leaders are taken up with rearranging deckchairs on a sinking ship, instead of manning the pumps, putting out the fires or doing whatever is necessary to establish the truthfulness of the Christian faith.

BUT WHAT ABOUT . . .

Now the one giant, and as yet unspoken, question mark that hangs over this approach to Christian leadership, whether it be parachurch, megachurch or small Christian mission organization, is the fact that the church is growing fastest in the non-Western world and that many of these churches, while almost exclusively theologically conservative, are also, let it be said, churches that emphasize the experiential.

Here is where, once again, we deal with the horns of the dilemma of a post-Enlightenment world. When we think of being "biblically intelligent," we tend to think in terms of being intellectual or highly educated. Non-Westerners rarely have such hang-ups. What is needed is Bible-soaked approaches to leadership. Experience is not the enemy of biblical intelligence, or should not be or need not be. Instead, a biblical intelligence rightly embraces experiential elements of the Christian faith. Edwards, none can gainsay, was an experientialist: he preached, encountered and believed in exciting and life-changing immediate experiences of God.

While these examples of rapidly growing churches in the non-Western world are a testimony to the importance of not downplaying the experiential aspects of Christianity, they are also a warning about the importance of the educative side of Christian ministry. For the great need in these churches, they themselves would say, is for more trained teachers and leaders. There is real danger of heresy. There is the tendency to run to extremes. And the devil so quickly thrown out by the means of experience may come back in by that same door as an angel of light urging all sorts of weird and wonderful practices in the name of Christianity, which a biblically intelligent leadership would know were wrong. It is already happening.

Once again we see the foresight and insight of Edwards' approach to ministry, leadership and the importance of biblical intelligence.

Is there anything, though, in this method that should be criticized? At the very least there is a potential misunderstanding against which we need to guard when we think of biblical intelligence as a primary need for effective leadership. When we hear a call for the Word to be taught, it is easy to turn it into an excuse to be always talking and never doing. The Bible makes it clear that "mere talk leads only to poverty" (Proverbs 14:23), and, as James puts it, we should not be like the person who looks in the mirror and then does nothing about it; not be hearers of the word only, but be doers as well (James 1:22–25).

This call to biblical intelligence is not a call to passivity: it is a call to action. Nor is it a call merely to intellectual action. At the very basic level, not all of us should be teachers (James 3:1). Only some have that difficult responsibility. If we are called by God to proclaim God's Word, in one form or another, that is no protection against the responsibility to obey his Word, but rather an increasing responsibility to do what we say others should do. We will be judged more harshly as teachers of the Word: James emphasizes that point. There is a tendency among those attracted to "teaching" not to be active in evangelism, strategic planning or any such apparently more "worldly" or more pragmatic activities. It is true there is a need for pastors who teach today, and for Christian leaders in whatever organization to be biblically intelligent leaders. But that is not the only vocation, nor is it the sum of a Christian's vocation as a Christian. We are to be parents for Christ, spouses for him; and the church needs activists, people who do God's Word, and not merely those who hear it and *do nothing*.

So there is a need for balance, as always. Nonetheless, part of the reason for the weakness in the Western church is that it has failed to generate, or give a sufficient public platform to, those who are able to proclaim God's Word credibly in an age in which there has been a systematic, sustained attack on the authority of that Word.

8.

HUMAN LEADERS FAIL

The in-flight magazine I was reading contained an article about the typical schedule of busy executives. "Often," it said, "busy executives will work up to sixty hours a week." Sixty hours? I thought to myself: I can't remember the last time I worked *only* sixty hours a week.

Many a leader struggles with such schedules. We demand personal charm, moral character and technical skill of the highest caliber of our public officers. It all takes a lot of time. And when we discover they have clay feet (they make mistakes!), our leaders quickly move from being heroes to being zeros. Yesterday's titans are today's delinquents.

WE ALL FAIL

Søren Kierkegaard went so far as to describe failure as the very heart of the Christian revelation. In his ground-breaking philosophical/theological oddity *The Sickness unto Death* (1941), Kierkegaard came to this conclusion on the basis of the traditional Christian view of sin. Our souls are naturally captive to an evil force, our sinful ego, ruled by the kingdom of darkness, and in direct rebellion against the kingdom of God. We all fail.

Once converted, of course, we are translated to the kingdom of light. Our hearts are regenerated. We are given works "prepared in advance for us to do" (Ephesians 2:10). None of us is a failure any more. We proceed from glory to glory and nothing can separate us from the love of God.

But it is also true, even as Christians, that we constantly fail. For the work of God in us is precisely that: the work of God. Our works are good works, honoring and glorifying to Christ, because they are Christ's works in us. We in our own selves are incapable of pleasing him, fallen and 'depraved' failures as we are. Yet in Christ, because of him and through him, we are able to rise to new heights of delightful achievement. We may even "aim for perfection," as the apostle Paul urges (2 Corinthians 13:11).

Yet we also remain failures. Paul was. Peter was. John was. I am. Jesus was not – and in him I rise to perfection, glory and eternal love; but in my own sinful self, whose influence in this life I never fully lose, I am nothing but an abject failure. Occasionally, even in the most eminent Christian, this "old man" emerges from his expulsion and we give in to temptation: we sin and fail. It happens to the best of us. There would be no need for the apostle John to write, "If we confess our sins, he is faithful and just and will forgive us our sins and purify us from all unrighteousness" (1 John 1:9), if it were not also true that "If we claim we have not sinned, we make him out to be a liar and his word has no place in our lives" (1 John 1:10).

People fall into two equal but opposite errors when they consider Christian heroes. The first is to paint them in such virulent, even vicious, terms that sainthood appears akin to insanity or even terrorism. Some of Edwards' less attractive traits have suffered at the hands of such surgical butchers. But, at the other extreme, it is possible to describe the virtues of our Christian heroes in such glowing terms that their achievements drift outside the realms of possibility, of this real gritty world, and into the realm of idol worship. It is not only Roman Catholics who are in danger of worshipping saints. Many a Protestant has a similar array of icons in his mind, even if the actual historical entities differ, and the means of worship is more subtle.

Somehow we must move beyond caricaturing our forebears either so negatively or so positively. Edwards did fail. It is just perhaps even more edifying for us to realize and learn from his errors as from his successes. Suddenly Edwards becomes human. And then his remarkable achievements are brought within the realm of possibility for other humans, like you and me.

EDWARDS AND SLAVERY

Edwards' view of slavery has recently become more widely attested. A previously unknown scrap of paper describes Edwards' notes for a presentation in defense of another local minister. This minister had got into trouble because he had a slave. Even then in New England some agitated for the freedom of slaves. Edwards was asked to prepare a response to defend the minister. He does so. Edwards advocating *for* slavery is not something most evangelicals would relish. Yet the fact remains.

It must be nuanced, however. First, Edwards was not a hierarchical religious chieftain. This is one of the most common caricatures today. As we have seen, Edwards in this view is portrayed as a representative of the old (perhaps "English") aristocracy, wearing his "wig" and being expelled from his pulpit because he refused to move with the democratic times soon to be exemplified in the War of Independence. Edwards' attitude to slavery becomes a piece of this classist puzzle.

However, the most revolutionary social movement of his day, the Great Awakening, was embraced by Edwards. While Edwards was no doubt a man of his time, and had traditional views about the authority of the clergy, it is excessive to paint as a classist repressive someone who used stories from simple members of his congregation in his books, who organized an "international concert of prayer," and who eagerly accepted Whitefield when the Boston elite rejected him. Versions of history that interpret everything as a class power struggle have become as nearly ubiquitous as the old "Whiggish" history, which was criticized for seeing everything in terms of the progress of Western-style parliamentary democracy.

Second, while Edwards did have an attitude to slavery unacceptable today (more about that later), his direct descendants were active in defeating, not defending, the slave trade. There is a theological time bomb in Edwards' thought and writing (as within the gospel itself) that ticked away during the middle of the eighteenth century and exploded later in the abolition of slavery throughout the British Empire, and eventually America too. Jonathan Edwards, Jr. was active in opposing slavery. So were many others who stood in Edwards' theological slipstream. Never was there a sense of discordance from Edwards' thinking and preaching in their opposition to slavery; rather of fulfillment and application.

Third, Edwards himself apparently opposed slavery in principle. It is true that the Edwards family seemed always to have had at least one slave. It is also true that Edwards defended slavery, as witnessed by the scrap of paper upon which are jotted some of Edwards' brief thoughts on the matter. Yet, even within this microcosm of his thinking, we find a principled opposition to African slavery. He felt it was despicable and inhumane to traffic in men, women and children, take them from their native country and import them to a foreign continent.

Fourth, until very recently in history (at Edwards' time), slavery had been a normal pattern of life for vast swathes of humanity. That does not make it right, but it does help explain why Edwards opposed African slavery in particular. Serfs and European versions of indentured bondage were common in European history.

Fifth, in Edwards' time, white servants had many of the same inhibition of rights as full-blown slaves. Servants were bonded to the family they served and could not marry without the permission of their master.

Once we put all these pieces together, once we contextualize Edwards' remarks, we begin to realize Edwards' attitude to slavery was not an example of his own basic evil principles, his hierarchical belief in the domination of white Christendom, or any such nonsense. Rather, I emphasize, Edwards wrongly supported slavery not *because* of his principles and the gospel but *in spite* of them. Edwards acted here against the principles of Christian freedom and justice, not in support of them. In fact, he acted in discordant disharmony with his own pastoral practice.

Communion in a Puritan church was a big deal. In our churches today we can take communion or the Lord's Supper pretty much anywhere, with no questions (normally) asked. For the Puritans communion was rightly guarded against those who did not partake of the Lord, and therefore should not participate in the Lord's Supper.

Now Edwards admitted African slaves into full membership of his church. They were not consigned to a subsection of the church, they did not become a specially targeted group within the membership, they did not even form their own "black" church. They were full members. They drank from the same cup. They ate the same loaf. They were one in Christ. This principle of the gospel – clearly articulated, understood and practiced by Edwards – was only later to gain rightful application to the issue of slavery. But it was there.

But what was Edwards' argument in favor of slavery? First, as I have said, he acknowledged the evil practice of African slavery and argued against that. His case for slavery was pragmatic. He stated it was impossible genuinely to do without slavery, because much of New England's produce came from plantations harvested by slaves. Edwards felt it was hypocritical to argue against slavery in New England and then buy sugar. That was the product of slavery too. In fact he felt it was impossible to escape the reality of slavery in his world, and so it was necessary to make the best of it. In fact, in many ways, the implication of his argument – brief and circumspect as it is on the scrap of paper – sounds somewhat similar to the kind of advice Paul gives slaves and masters in the New Testament. Be a good slave, he says. Be a good master, he says. Remember, you have a master in heaven (Ephesians 6:5–9).

That does not mean the New Testament is "pro-slavery." It does mean that in social settings where revolutionary change is not possible it is *at the least* required of Christians to act in an honest, peaceable and effective way, serving the Lord. The New Testament sees beyond this. We are all one in Christ (Ephesians 2:15). Philemon should be freed, Paul says, 'no longer as a slave, but better than a slave, as a dear brother' (Philemon 1:16). The principle within Edwards' theology and practice similarly looked beyond, though its implications were wrongly not applied. Just a few decades after his death evangelical leaders, including Edwards' followers, such as Samuel Hopkins and Jonathan Edwards, Jr., began to champion the anti-slavery movement.

So we need to have balanced and nuanced appreciation of the historical context of Edwards' remarks. Nonetheless, the Edwards family commonly had at least one slave ("Rose" was one) and there are records of Sarah Edwards seeking to buy a slave. Despite the understandable caution and social context in which Edwards was placed, we might have expected better than this from him. As a human leader Edwards here failed, though the gospel he preached pointed to implications beyond his own grasp.

EDWARDS AND PASTORAL CARE

But this short-sightedness was not the only human failing Edwards expressed. Jonathan Edwards was an unusual character. The much-reported statistic of his spending thirteen hours in his study does not fully describe Edwards' daily regime, which was also punctuated by frequent pastoral visitors, twice-daily family devotions, regular and appreciated interruptions from his wife, and the habit of taking his children with him on pastoral trips. Edwards was not the academic loner the thirteen-hours-a-day-in-his-study depiction suggests. Nonetheless, he did list towards the academic and doctrinal as opposed to the relational and personal. We have already discussed the reasons for Edwards' ejection from his pulpit. The substance of these was principled: Edwards objected to the compromised church polity against which he began to teach and preach. By and large in the midst of this controversy he handled himself in an exemplary manner.

However, he did make mistakes. Some of the tension that arose during the "Communion Controversy" was no doubt due to Edwards' own personal habits of distance and lack of personal contact with his congregation. Reading the debate, one gets the sense that some of the disagreements could have been ironed out fairly easily between well-meaning and open-minded friends. Along the way, however, Edwards had become elevated from his congregation, distant from them, and when a controversial issue emerged, there was neither the web of relationships nor the investment in personal capital that might have made the disagreements less emotionally charged.

In particular Edwards appears to have mishandled the "bad book case." Some young people were caught reading a midwife's guide in a barn, in a day when pornographic literature was rather harder to come by. The people were shocked. It was a difficult situation, for some of the young people were children of the most influential members of the congregation. Edwards decided to level the playing field by calling publicly all of the young people to meet with him after church. The trouble was, given the now charged fear of accusation running through several families, this was interpreted as Edwards tarring all of the young people with the same brush. Even those perfectly innocent were publicly named and shamed – or at least so it was felt. One empathizes with Edwards in this situation. Pastoral judgments like these are notoriously tricky, and a bit more charity on the part of the families would have avoided any offence being taken. Still, perhaps a private counsel with those caught in the act rather than a public – perceived – rebuke of all, innocent or guilty, might have been rather more prudent. In the midst of the Communion Controversy, this misjudged pastoral decision was one from which perhaps Edwards never recovered.

EDWARDS AND DOCTRINE

I do not agree with all of Edwards' theological framework. In substance I could not be closer; with many of the peripheral issues I am one with him; but on some matters I think he was mistaken. I also think some of these are directly related to the crisis of the Communion Controversy, his ejection from the pulpit, and maybe even the inability to see beyond his anaemic criticism of African slavery.

Edwards was a Puritan New England Congregationalist. He held, as we have seen, to infant baptism. Many today, rightly or wrongly, believe the New Testament teaches believer's baptism, but that infant versus believer's baptism is not a substantial matter of the gospel: it affects only the polity and practice of a local church. In fact Edwards wrestled with the implications of infant baptism. Penned at the end of a long private note in a later hand are the words "these things about baptism be doubtful." More to the point, his change in opinion during the Communion Controversy was not only about communion; it was also about baptism. He wished now that only those who professed personal faith in Jesus, who alone could be allowed into full communicant membership, could have their children baptized. This was an attempt to take the church back to being a gathered body of genuine believers, rather than a social representation of the upstanding citizens of the town. This was revolutionary! But it was not entirely new, for many of the Puritans had left Old England precisely because of their disgust at the "mixed" nature of the established church. Yet by the eighteenth century the Puritan Congregational church in New England had become the new establishment, and Edwards' doctrine of the necessity of conversion to share in the benefits of church membership was bound to ruffle feathers, to put it mildly.

Baptists may wonder whether, if more Puritans, and the magisterial Reformation in general, had consistently applied their understanding of the gospel and the church to baptism, Edwards would not have got into the mess he did. The radical Reformation understood the need for consistency in this area, but they might feel too few were Reformed Baptists, and of them too few had at this stage social or ecclesiastical influence. There was Roger Williams, and the First London Baptist Confession of the early seventeenth century, but it was not until the Victorian era that a leader of the influence of a Spurgeon emerged.

So Edwards' theology of the church was not perfect. His too-structured view of church and of social order in general may have made it difficult for him to envisage a social revolution along class lines.

In the main, Edwards' theology of personal spiritual experience is stunningly useful and insightful pastorally and individually. I cannot think of a better start to ministerial training than a careful perusal of Edwards' *Religious Affections,* or a more pertinent balm to the shallow commercialized experiences of many a churchgoer today. Yet, as mentioned earlier, he believed the miraculous gifts of the Spirit had ceased with the apostolic age. Much of his opposition to the radical Great Awakening came as he feared the beginning of "enthusiasm," the unwarranted trust in personal spiritual hunches in opposition to or removal of Scripture. To follow such intuitions, Edwards felt, was like leaving the guidance of the pole star to follow a "Jack with a lantern."

To this we must all – whether cessationist or not – say "Amen." Too much damage has been done to the church by "angels of light" claiming to provide new revelation in addition to the Scriptures. However, since Jonathan Edwards, several important subdistinctions have been made with regard to the theology of charismatic gifts. Wayne Grudem and others have taught us to see that it is, at least, possible to hold to a charismatic theology of the spiritual gifts while not believing that "prophecy" or "words of knowledge" are in any way authoritative over the life of faith. You may not agree with Grudem, but Edwards did not envisage this kind of careful textual work done within his own Reformed tradition, one allowing for a high view of Scripture and the centrality of Bible teaching in worship, while accepting a place for spiritual insights of a more subjective nature. With the exponential growth of the non-Western church, much of which is fuelled by the Pentecostal or charismatic movements, it becomes hard to shut one's eyes to at least a measure of God's blessing.

IS IT RIGHT TO CRITICIZE A MAN OF GOD?

What more can we criticize Edwards for? It almost seems unfair to point out blemishes on a man of God. We certainly should not be among those who take delight in uncovering clay feet. Neither, however, are we to pretend that weaknesses do not exist, or be surprised when we find them. Dietrich Bonhoeffer, another hero for many, remarked once that what we need is not more spiritual superheroes but more spiritual servants. It is the seventh of his principles for eradicating selfish ambition in the fellowship:

> Jesus made authority in the fellowship dependent upon brotherly service (Mark 10:43) . . . Every cult of personality that emphasizes the distinguished qualities, virtues, and talents of another person, even though these be of an altogether spiritual nature, is worldly and has no place in the Christian community; indeed, it poisons the Christian community . . . Genuine authority realizes that it can exist only in the service of Him who alone has authority . . . The Church does not need brilliant personalities but faithful servants of Jesus and the brethren . . . Pastoral authority can be attained only by the servant of Jesus who seeks no power of his own, who himself is a brother among brothers to the authority of the Word. (D. Bonhoeffer, *Life Together* [New York: Harper & Row, 1954])

Our admiration for Edwards must not become adoration, nor must it descend to a "cult of personality." In fact, the very process of noticing failings and shortfalls exalts the Lord Jesus Christ, who used Edwards. It disentangles the man from the Master.

The Bible is far more realistic about human heroes than many a pious biography. Even that roll call of biblical heroes, Hebrews 11, points out their faith, not their full perfection. Delving into the Old Testament reveals that God used a liar (Abraham), a murderer (Moses), an adulterer (David) and an occasional depressive (Elijah). The New Testament similarly records God's hand not only upon a simple fisherman (Peter) but also a religious terrorist (Paul, or, as he was then, Saul). This is not to dissuade us from following their example. Paul frequently urges his disciples to imitate him. But there is a caveat. As Paul puts it, "Follow my example, as I follow the example of Christ" (1 Corinthians 11:1). That is not only a command to obey and model your life upon the apostle's; it is also a statement about the extent and boundaries of that imitation. We are to follow Paul to the extent that he follows Christ.

146

Similar parameters pertain for Edwards. If anything, of course, our imitation of him must be severely less than our imitation of Paul, and even that only as a means to the imitation of Christ. To achieve that mixture of humble learning yet appropriate focus upon Jesus, it is necessary to point out not only what is worthy of imitation but also what is not. They may be pimples on an otherwise beautiful visage, but we are to aim to become beautiful, not adopt the pimples in an unworthy imitation of the lesser subject.

So often we miss this. Our mentors' idiosyncrasies are copied, while their heart for Jesus is forgotten. We pick up on their style, upon their diction, upon their mannerisms. We notice what makes them stick out from the rest – their unusual or imbalanced opinions. Unconsciously we adopt those peripheral matters in a selfishly ambitious attempt to aspire to their eminence, all the while missing out on the source of their power and effectiveness: the hidden presence of the Lord Jesus Christ himself. They are just jars of clay with an all-surpassing power from God.

DO THIS – DON'T DO THAT

There are three things not to do that Edwards did, and four things to *do better* that Edwards did well.

1. As a pastor, Edwards modeled *passive* pastoral care. That is, he attended to the needs of his flock when they sought him out and asked for help. In contrast, the Puritan Richard Baxter modeled *proactive* pastoral care. He set up a rigorous and detailed pastoral visitation system whereby everyone in the town was regularly trained at a personal level by the pastor himself. This took hard work and was quite demanding. But Edwards had good reasons for avoiding personal visitation. He felt he was singularly gifted at preaching and writing, and particularly bad at turning informal conversations to spiritually profitable ends. In this regard Edwards' personal judgment may well have been acute. Nonetheless, the charge of the pastor to take care of the flock requires personal, proactive contact, whether of the traditional

visitation kind or setting up appointments over coffee or lunch. Edwards did not do this. He was passive in pastoral care, when pastors need to be proactive in pastoral care. Their visiting or more general personal skills may be less than brilliant, but even a shaky conversation on general matters not precisely connected to the gospel is preparation work for the ministry of the Word on a Sunday.

2. Edwards introduced a changed principle of practice within his church later in his ministry, and to the surprise of his parishioners. He may well have been right about this principle in every respect, and we may even think he could easily have gone further. But in the method of his introduction there was cause for offence, even if the substance of his case were to be accepted. His parishioners could readily have felt the wool had been pulled over their eyes when Edwards began to change things so late in his ministry.

Pastors change their opinions, as anyone else does, and we might even hope that they will do so in relation to more light gleaned from Scripture. But the method of introduction of such changes needs to be sensitive, humble and not "lecturing" in style. A gentle answer turns away wrath, and a patient word can break a bone. But lengthy treatises, however brilliant and sparkling with intellectual insight, are likely to be a turn-off, unless the groundwork of agreement has first been laid more personally and privately.

In other words, Edwards introduced change suddenly and aggressively, when we should introduce it gradually and carefully. There are, these days, whole strategies on managing change in church. It is an important subject, for none of us likes to change. It is true that the gospel is essentially a word of "change," requiring as it does not only a one-time repentance but a continual growth in godliness. Nonetheless, wise Christian leaders will manage change humbly and be considerate of the weakness and frailty of most people in the face of new circumstances.

3. Edwards attempted to have an implicitly baptistic ecclesiastical policy within an explicitly Congregationalist polity. This too was not a great idea. But what do I mean by an 'implicitly baptistic policy'?

Edwards' view that only converted people, who professed personal faith and regeneration, could be members and could take communion, and that only their children could be baptized, was not an explicitly baptistic policy. He held throughout his life to infant baptism. But the rationale that persuaded him of the need for a genuinely gathered community of real Christians – the clear New Testament vision, not the vision of Constantinian Christianity – could only really logically be expressed within a baptistic framework.

The New England Congregationalist Puritans gradually discovered this in practice, if not in recognition of the fact. Steadily, those who had been real Christians gave birth to those who were then baptized and included because of their baptism within the church; some of them were later converted when of an age to profess faith, but others were not, as is the way of grace. What to do with these baptized but unconverted members?

Stoddard, Edwards' grandfather and predecessor in the Northampton pulpit, invented a creative solution. Edwards realized, though, that allowing unconverted members to take communion was beyond the pale, and gradually the whole system in his mind began to unravel. Particularly, as he said, with regard to baptism (letter to Thomas Foxcroft, 24 May 1749):

> My people, in length of time and with great difficulty, might be brought to yield the point as to the qualifications for the Lord's Supper, though that is very uncertain. But with respect to the other sacrament [Baptism], there is scarce any hope of it. And this will be very likely to overthrow me, not only with regard to my usefulness in the work of the ministry here, but everywhere. (J. E. Smith, H. S. Stout and K. P. Minkema [eds.], *A Jonathan Edwards Reader* [Yale University Press, 1995], p. 309)

The reason why there was "scarce any hope" that his view about baptism would prevail was that established practice conflicted with this (apparently) new principle. The accepted ecclesiastical practice, especially the halfway covenant of Solomon Stoddard's compromise, conflicted with the principle Edwards now wanted to establish regarding baptism and church membership. Some would even say that within the basic system of congregational Puritanism there was an essential conflict along these lines. To preach regeneration and a gathered community of saints *at the same time* as admitting into communicant membership all the baptized children of church members is storing up trouble.

For Stoddard to solve this dilemma by defining communion as a "converting ordinance" is fixing a San Andreas Fault with glue. Then, for Edwards to insist (against the honored example of his predecessor Stoddard) on evidence of regeneration for all members is practically begging the nuclear reactor to go critical. This essential conflict between gospel principle and ecclesiastical practice may be clearer for us to spot today than at perhaps any other time in the West, as we move from a "Christendom" understanding of Christianity to a post-Constantine appreciation for the original spirit of the New Testament texts.

We must be careful to ensure that our gospel principles are reflected in our church structures. If there is a basic conflict between the message we preach and the ecclesiastical form in which it is preached, there will be at some point – whether in our generation or that to come – an explosion. We cannot put new wine in old wine skins. There must be a reflection of the radical, root and branch, principle of regeneration in the structure of the church. If we say only those who have personally experienced grace are members of God's church, then our structures need to ensure that, as much as possible, and, in the judgment of charity, only those who have experienced grace are members of our churches. Edwards inherited a situation where grace was proclaimed and experienced but where the ecclesiastical system allowed, implicitly, non-converted members of local churches to be accepted and gain influence. No wonder he had such a tough time after the Great Awakening.

Those, then, are the three things to do that Edwards did not do (or inherited as not done). Edwards had a passive approach to pastoral care; we should have an active approach. Edwards introduced change late in the day and suddenly; we are to introduce change openly, steadily and carefully. Edwards inherited a situation in which the gospel was encased, not expressed, in the ecclesiastical structure; we need to encourage our church administration to reflect our Christian message.

There are also four things Edwards did well that we could do better.

1. *Edwards was a great preacher.* Can we do better? We can certainly do more than merely imitate his stylistic idiosyncrasies. Preaching wanes when it slavishly copies the style of famous preachers. The well-attuned ear can hear the stylistic "tics" that are tell-tale signs of influential preaching mentors. Edwards' Reformed style of preaching can be imitated – the heavy doctrine – without its spirit being expressed. Edwards was actually very practical in his preaching. Unlike some "Reformed" preachers who look to Edwards as their model, he was someone who integrated exposition with practical application. There were extensive "uses" to his sermons that take up pages of the detailed sermon notes he has bequeathed us. We need to find the spirit of the preaching, not the letter of the sermon.

2. *Edwards was a missionary.* Edwards, when he had been expelled from his pulpit, went to be a missionary to the Stockbridge Indians. Edwards, as already mentioned, also wrote the groundbreaking missionary biography of David Brainerd, which inspired David Livingstone, Hudson Taylor, William Carey and many other nineteenth-century pioneering missionaries. Edwards was a great supporter of missions and the vision of a global church.

We can do better. We have more resources and a greater sense of the need for mission in the furthermost corners of the globe. We have far less excuse to be "Eurocentric" in our understanding of Christianity, living as we do in a time of massive growth in Christianity in the East, South America and Africa. Edwards' mission vision reached far, but ours should reach farther still.

3. *Edwards was a creative apologist for the orthodox Christian faith.* This in an age of intellectual assault on the foundations of the Bible. He was expert at this. He integrated apologetics into much of his preaching. He made extensive arguments for the rationality and truthfulness of the Christian faith.

Again, we can do better, for we have more resources. Indeed, we must do better, for the attack upon the historicity of the Bible and veracity of the exclusive claims of Christ have reached depths unthought of by Edwards.

4. *Edwards was an advocate of mass prayer meetings.* His "concert of prayer," as we have seen, was an idea of Christian people from all over the world gathering together at the same time on the same day to seek God's face for revival. In our era of mass communication, surely this is an idea whose time has come. As our churches become more business-orientated, as we learn more techniques for getting people to come to our church, for marketing church and for church growth, we forget the lessons of history and geography.

Historically the church has grown fastest and made its most dramatic inroads into the world in response to the urgent prayers of God's people. *Geographically* too, the parts of the church growing fastest have frequent and extensive prayer for revival. Not to mention the scriptural promise "If my people, who are called by my name, will humble themselves and pray and seek my face and turn from their wicked ways, then will I hear from heaven and will forgive their sin and will heal their land" (2 Chronicles 7:14).

The bottom line is that our heroes are only pointers to the true hero: Christ himself. He stands head in the clouds above all. Not only that, but the very failings God allows in our human heroes are designed by him to ensure we keep our eyes focused on the real source of all blessing and the only man worthy of worship: Christ Jesus, the incarnate Son of God.

FAMILY LIFE
AND EFFECTIVE MINISTRY
ARE RECONCILABLE

Only after they had had a new glass-fronted skyscraper constructed did the owners of the building discover that those seated near the windows felt unnerved by the thought of nothing but glass between them and a scary drop. Eventually, the owners decided to call in an engineer to explain the manufactured strength of this special glass. The engineer walked on to the floor where the office workers had congregated, noticed them all sitting a long way from the glass wall, arms crossed, faces portraying a "Don't think you can change my mind" attitude, and decided on the spur of the moment to switch tactics. He dropped his clipboard stacked with facts and statistics, backed up to the farthest point from the glass window and began to run as fast as he could towards the glass. He then took a flying leap at the window and bounced back unharmed, except for a somewhat bruised shoulder.

There was a momentary silence from the office workers, and then a communally murmured, "Oh." No-one minded sitting next to the glass after that. When we say, "Family life and effective ministry are reconcilable," many a contemporary minister will respond, "You must be joking!" Edwards' example of home life is worth considering, because it helps demolish the stereotype.

PRESSURES ON PASTORS TODAY

To those in the working world, being on staff at a church might appear something of a cushy ride. We understandably assume the pressures of pastoral ministry are much less than, say, corporate finance or management consulting. Surely, we think, it is a wonderful privilege to spend our day with other Christians rather than among the negative influences of secular culture. Is it not marvelous to be paid to read the Bible and explain it to others? Which Christian would not feel a warm glow at having prayer as a large part of their working day? How lovely it would be to work for the church rather than a cut-throat boss.

There is truth to this belief in the privilege of being a full-time pastoral employee of a local church. Pastors frequently feel this sense of honored opportunity. They sometimes talk of their "calling," which expresses not only select circumstance, but also a personal belief in a commission from the Almighty. When they walk up the steps to their pulpit on Sunday mornings, they know they are about to deliver the "oracles of God." Rare indeed is the biblical pastor who does not have an immeasurable delight in being able to invest his working life in an eternal heritage.

Yet there is another side to the matter. Pastors today uniformly describe intense working pressure. Contemporary surveys record the kind of employment headaches we might have thought were the sole preserve of aggressive business culture. I am even told that a growing number of pastors seriously contemplate suicide.

Such a depressing attitude may seem incredible, given the other advantages already described. It would be tempting to diagnose these feelings as a sign of spiritual immaturity, or being spoilt: even honey tastes nauseous to those who eat too much. Yet the breadth of the reality of these pressures cannot be dismissed.

PERSONAL ILLUSTRATIONS

Perhaps a few examples will help. While finishing this section of the book, I have had the following challenges. I have had a book signing for another book. I have preached. I have had two articles to write. I have had one long denominational meeting. I have had several other long church leadership meetings. I have two major pastoral issues to solve, along with all the more normal pastoral matters to minister within. I have had the ongoing run of staff and elders meetings, plus preparation for an elders' day retreat. It has been my wife's birthday. An old friend has arrived. My son continues to struggle with autism. My daughter is thriving but needs attention. This coming weekend I have three sermons to prepare and a section in a book to finish (you guessed which!).

We also need to locate a new worship space for our church in the next couple of months. I had an interview for someone's term paper today. A local newspaper wants me to comment on something; someone has a personal issue; a baptismal interview; several "interesting" phone calls, and so on. There are also nineteen potential new members to follow up after our introductory membership class.

That is a pretty typical schedule. I have left some things out. You need to fill in the blanks a little. In particular, add the emotional intensity of pastoral ministry. Chatting to a friend who's recently left the ministry and is now doing a "normal" job, he tells me he cannot believe how short eight-hour days are. He says now he goes home and that's the end of it. He doesn't have to think about work at home. There's no "burden" for the church, the burden Paul considered more onerous than physical beatings (2 Corinthians 11:28).

Generally speaking, pastors face the pressure of wanting to please God and yet being employed by people, and needing to function appropriately within human accountability structures. When my wife and I were looking seriously at one pastoral job opening, I knew I had to give a clear account of my biblical views on a certain doctrinal matter, which I also knew would sink my candidacy. That's an intense example, especially as we had no other source of income at the time. But that need to please God (which sometimes means displeasing God's people: look at Moses!) carries a weight beyond normal job expectations.

Discussing these pressures with the ministry staff at our church, we discovered that the forms of pressure varied. One simply mentioned the massive amount to get done. Another talked in terms of being overwhelmed by expectations if an event seemed to go poorly, or proud feelings if things went well. Someone else spoke of the special difficulties of being responsible for communication in a complex organism such as a church. There were some comments about the pressures of clearly establishing priorities, both among the ministry tasks themselves and also between the ministry and home life. It was remarked how difficult it is to balance the needs or desires of the teams we coordinate versus the importance of casting vision and establishing healthy leadership.

None of us was by any means suicidal, or depressed, and all were grateful for the thriving church it is our privilege (that word comes naturally) to serve. Yet it would be untrue to say we did not feel pressure.

BIBLICAL PRECEDENTS

Of course, even a skim-reading of Paul's letters to his protégés Timothy and Titus would prove that pressure in pastoral ministry is not an exclusively modern phenomenon. Paul urged young Timothy to be strong, to be like an athlete and soldier, to let no-one look down on his youth, to encourage and rebuke with all authority, to avoid getting entangled in foolish arguments. Timothy was to be made aware of the fact that people will be lovers of themselves, selfish, slanderous and worse. Some would worm their way into homes and gain control over the weak-willed, spoiling the house fellowships. Just as Moses was opposed, so Timothy would be opposed.

Opposition to Timothy required gentle instruction in the hope that God would bring the opponents to repentance and that they would thus escape the trap of the devil, who had taken them captive to do his will. Not only was Timothy commanded to preach the word and do the work of an evangelist, but he was also instructed to endure hardship. He was to be a soldier, an athlete and a farmer, professions not known for their easy lifestyle. Timothy needed to be reminded that God had given him a spirit not of timidity but of power, love and self-discipline.

Titus, meanwhile, had a pastoral charge in Crete, where Paul was ready to agree with one of their local poets that the people there were evil brutes and lazy gluttons. Titus had to appoint elders so they could refute those who opposed sound doctrine, as there were many rebellious people. He needed to be told to warn a divisive person once, then again, and then have nothing to do with him. At the end stood the example of Paul, who was being poured out like a drink offering, whose departure was coming near, and who had fought the good fight, finished the race and kept the faith. Pastoral ministry, according to the Pastoral Epistles, is no easy ride. If those on church staff could tell Paul what they were going through today he would not feel surprised. Biblical ministry has always been tough.

WHAT'S CHANGED

A cultural shift has added fuel to the flame: we are moving out of a stage of being the "Christian West." There may be strategic advantages to this change that will gradually emerge. It may be helpful to disentangle the gospel from Western Christian nominalism. It may serve the cause of the church well that now the largest component of Christians is in the developing world. Still, the removal of Western "Christendom" as a historical reality means that other pressures are brought to bear emotionally, spiritually and practically.

Emotionally, while in the West the office of Christian ministry has for hundreds of years been held in respect (at least theoretically), these days that attitude no longer pertains. It is hard to work in a role whose very existence is viewed as an epitome of archaic cultural redundancy. *Spiritually,* while for many years churches took it for granted that people would come to church regularly, to make that assumption now is courting disaster. It is hard to shoulder the burden not just of shepherding but of mission as well. And *practically,* while the salary and resources of the pastor have until recently been commensurate with at least a low-end professional salary (and at times that of a well-paid position), nowadays many pastors are paid minimally. It is hard to be constrained by the practical necessity of bivocational life or needing other investments to pay bills when also under these kinds of pastoral pressures.

In other words, as the respect and resources for the pastoral ministry have declined in the West, *at the same time* the demands and dilemmas have increased. These are the rock and the hard place between which many pastors live.

Take all this and combine it with family life. Some day it would make an interesting study to observe when the term "PK" emerged. PK stands for "Pastor's Kid," but often implies emotional issues connected to fatherly neglect. I would not be surprised if the syndrome was first noticed at the same time as these (post)modern pressures on pastors began.

EDWARDS' MODEL

What can we do? Here is where Edwards' example helps. Certainly he lived at a time when the salary of the pastor was relatively far higher, and where the pastor was a more respected part of his society. However, he also had his pressures. Gradually, during his ministry, a pastor was becoming one of the leading figures of a town. What is more, Edwards had a busy and demanding ministry. Granted (unlike most today) he had several servants and helpers to release him from spending time doing the dishes; nonetheless, some of the principles he modeled are worthy of our attention and emulation.

First, it is important to realize the extent of Edwards' family commitments: he had eleven children, and ten lived to adulthood. In any day, and under any circumstances, ten children to raise, feed and nurture is a massive responsibility. Sarah was by all accounts a remarkable woman, industrious in her approach to family and managing the home, efficient and effective in rearing the children. Much of the success of Edwards' children is no doubt due to her hard work and abilities.

Second, we should also note the remarkable long-term influence of Edwards' progeny. Al Sanders in the 1961 film *Crisis in Morality*! recounts the investigation into Jonathan and Sarah Edwards' descendants:

> An investigation was made of 1,394 known descendants of Jonathan Edwards of which 13 became college presidents, 65 college professors, 3 United States senators, 30 judges, 100 lawyers, 60 physicians, 75 army and navy officers, 100 preachers and missionaries, 60 authors of prominence, one a vice-president of the United States, 80 became public officials in other capacities, 295 college graduates, among whom were governors of states and ministers to foreign countries. His descendants did not cost the state a single penny.
> 'The memory of the just is blessed' (Prov. 10:7).

This is a different kind of PK! How did Edwards succeed, where we fail?

He had a church that implicitly understood the pastoral calling. Most churches today interpret the role of the pastor either as an educational role (like a teacher or academic) or as a business role (like a chief executive officer). Salaries are connected to either academic roles or CEO roles, and job descriptions and expectations tend to be formed by one or other of these common models in our contemporary consciousness. In Edwards' day there was an implicit understanding of what it meant to be distinctly pastoral in vocation – it had its own terms of reference and meaning.

This is a great need. Too often, pastors' expectations are shaped by employment cultures inimical to healthy working patterns in the pastorate. Someone needs to take down the letter of Paul to Timothy and Titus, shape them into a legal document, and serve that as a model for what is expected of pastors today. There would, if that were done, be not only an emphasis upon preparing to preach and pastoral work, but also the necessary authority invested in the pastor ("Encourage and rebuke with all authority," Titus 2:15) and encouragement to take care of himself and his family.

Edwards, though busy, nurtured a healthy relationship with his wife. He would spend many hours in his study, working long and hard. Yet the marriage between Jonathan and Sarah Edwards was famously sweet. George Whitefield noted when he visited the Edwards' manse what a household of peace it was, and resolved that he himself would get married. At the end of Edwards' life, when he lay on his deathbed, Jonathan asked that this powerfully affectionate message be given to his wife, for she was absent: tell her that our "uncommon union . . . has been of such a nature, as I trust is spiritual, and therefore will continue for ever" (G. Marsden, *Jonathan Edwards* [Yale University Press, 2003], p. 494). For a pious woman who reflects on Jesus' teaching that marriage is for this life only, few words could have been more comforting, or more descriptive of the rich, spiritual fabric out of which the cloth of their marriage had been carefully woven.

To create this secure texture to his marriage in a demanding ministry context, Jonathan Edwards first of all married the right woman. Sarah was undoubtedly a godly, effective, affectionate and exemplary wife in all sorts of ways. It is true that she suffered later criticism at the hands of Jonathan's Northampton opponents, who accused her of spending too much money on frivolities such as clothes. By that time, however, if either Jonathan or Sarah had blown their nose too much or too loudly it would have been used as fodder for the growing assault: such attacks on Sarah are evidence not of profound materialistic character flaws but of the relational dysfunction that had been created for other reasons. Sarah was such an example of godliness that Jonathan famously used her personal testimony to a revival-renewing experience as a model of what he was looking for as the ideal spiritual experience during the Great Awakening (Marsden, *Jonathan Edwards*, p. 240).

Their relationship, though, was not just due to a providentially accurate match-making choice, nor only to Sarah's long-standing piety. Jonathan was committed to the welfare of their love. Some have suggested that romantic love was the creation of the nineteenth century. But anyone who picks up the Bible and reads "Song of Songs" must surely attest to a rather longer history of romance in the human race. Even the end of Genesis 2 ("She is now bone of my bones, and flesh of my flesh") is rightly described as the first example of human love poetry.

Jonathan invested in this love. He was himself an affectionate man (witness his *Religious Affections* and many other works on the importance as well as correct place of emotions in religious life). He channeled this affection towards his wife. Perhaps, being the only boy of many girls when he grew up, he had a better-than-average grasp of what it took to communicate with a woman. He also established practical boundaries: his study was a place he occupied for long hours, but contemporary witnesses attest to Sarah's freedom of access to the study, and their peaceful, harmonious and generally idyllic relationship.

We could say, then, simply that Jonathan Edwards was not a workaholic. He was not addicted to work, or to ministerial success, but to God, and God is the only being worthy of our healthy worship. In that context, while Jonathan Edwards clocked up more than his fair share of long hours in ministerial labors, there was apparently always a sweetness to their relationship. He made time for Sarah, and Sarah in turn knew that any sacrifices she made were not for the ego of her husband but for the glory of God. Although the spiritual development of children is often seen to be the role and task of the mother, Edwards was deeply involved in nurturing his children spiritually. Edwards, in a classically Puritan way, took Ephesians 6:4, which speaks of the responsibility of fathers to "bring [their children] up in the training and instruction of the Lord," literally. Fathers have a responsibility to nurture their children spiritually. Given Jonathan Edwards' busy schedule, heavy pastoral demands and many other matters that could have occupied his attention, it would have been easy for him to delegate this task to another – perhaps another children's worker, or at least to his wife.

Principally this was accomplished through a systematic scheduling of each day. Jonathan led the family devotions. In some Christian circles today family devotions are deemed anachronistic, boring and likely to be a turn-off to true Christian commitment from children in the long term. In others a certain form of family devotions becomes a benchmark for the true piety of the family under the spotlight. The reality is that, given our varied and different schedules, the form of family devotions may differ, but the substance of fathers training their children in spiritual matters remains essential.

In addition to scheduling family devotions (yes devotions in the plural) each day, and keeping to that pattern, Jonathan Edwards also involved his children in his own spiritual work. When he traveled, he frequently took one of his children with him. These were opportunities for spiritual nurture and discussion, as well as for building the psychologically necessarily intimate relationship between father and child. Children love going out into the world with their parents – being protected by their dad, and being shown how to do simple tasks in everyday life. Coupling this psychological and practical necessity with spiritual discussion and conversation is a recipe for maximum spiritual investment in children. As Moses said, "Impress them [these commandments] on your children. Talk about them when you sit at home and when you walk along the road, when you lie down and when you get up" (Deuteronomy 6:7). In other words, in the midst of life, bring in spiritual direction. Jonathan Edwards did that too.

This was the basic framework of Edwards' approach to family life: a well-chosen spouse, a nurtured relationship with his wife and personal systematic, as well as informal, investment in the spiritual well-being of his children.

SOME EXAMPLES

Several personal writings of Jonathan Edwards pull back the curtain a little on this intimate world of the Edwards household. When Jonathan was still single, he wrote this love poem to Sarah, penned about 1723 (they married in 1727). Note how his clear affection for her is threaded through with an admiration for her spiritual qualities:

They say there is a young lady in [New Haven] who is beloved of
that almighty Being, who made and rules the world, and that there
are certain seasons in which this great Being, in some way or other
invisible, comes to her and fills her mind with exceeding sweet
delight, and that she hardly cares for anything, except to meditate
on him – that she expects after a while to be received up where he
is, to be raised out of the world and caught up into heaven; being
assured that he loves her too well to let her remain at a distance
from him always. There she is to dwell with him, and be lavished
with his love and delight always . . . (J. E. Smith, H. S. Stout and K.
P. Minkema [eds.], *A Jonathan Edwards Reader* [Yale University
Press, 1995], p. 281)

So it carries on. A literary critic would remark on how the spiritual
language is breathed through with a personal romantic edge. Perhaps
Edwards at this stage was also wanting to lavish his own love upon this
remarkable lady from New Haven. Nonetheless, that – in a way – is
precisely the point. Jonathan Edwards fell in love with Sarah because of,
not in spite of, her love for the Almighty. Marriage itself is not merely
an excuse for romantic observations: a rather later letter to Sarah
Edwards has a good deal more of the practical about it.

Sarah is away tending the Edwards' great long-time supporter,
Colonel Stoddard, who is lying on his deathbed. Jonathan writes,
describing the mild illnesses of his large household. He remarks that
"we have been without you almost as long as we know how to be." Yet he
also wishes to remind Sarah of more minor domestic matters: "If you
have money to spare, and it isn't too late, I should be glad if you would
buy us some cheese in Boston, and [send it] with other things if it can
be safely." Such practicalities of the marriage relationship do not escape
Jonathan (or Sarah) Edwards. Nonetheless, it is far from mechanical.
She is his "dear companion" and he, her "most affectionate companion"
(Smith, Stout and Minkema, *Jonathan Edwards Reader*, pp. 306–307).

Jonathan Edwards' concern for the well-being of his children is
expressed in one tender letter to his recently married daughter, Esther.
Esther Edwards married Rev. Aaron Burr, who was pastor of the

Newark, New Jersey, Presbyterian Church and president of the College of New Jersey. They married in 1752. By the next year, March 1753, Esther was experiencing some physical ailment, a trial to her and a test of the love of her husband. Jonathan's letter to his daughter on this occasion is full of unsentimental fatherly advice, parental affection and appropriate respect for her new husband. Here are some excerpts:

> Dear Child: We are glad that you are in any respect better, but concerned at your remaining weakness. I am glad . . . that you have experienced some inward divine consolations under your afflic-tion, by the extreme weakness and distressing pains, you have been the subject of. For these you ought to be thankful, and also for that unwearied kindness and tender care of your companion [Rev. Aaron Burr], which you speak of. (Smith, Stout and Minkema, Jonathan Edwards Reader, pp. 311–312)

Edwards then goes on pastorally to explain to Esther that she should not think her illness is anything strange, but merely one of the instances of what it means to live in this fallen world. He advises her that God is using this to teach her not to expect joy or hope in this world, but to put her hope in heaven. He counsels that she cannot expect to be restored to her family (the Edwards family) but, instead, "'Tis of infinitely more importance to have the presence of an heavenly Father, and to make progress towards an heavenly home. Let us all take care that we meet there at last" (Smith, Stout and Minkema, *Jonathan Edwards Reader*, p. 312).

These little pastoral necessities – urging Esther to put her trust in her heavenly Father rather than ultimately her human father – evidence the great affection and respect in which Edwards was held by his children.

Edwards, though, is not merely "pastoral": he is also parental. We might not agree with all his and Sarah's medical remedies, but there is no doubt that they were concerned for the practical well-being of their daughter! "As to means for your health, we have procured one rattle-snake, which is all we could get. It is a medicine that has been very ser-viceable to you heretofore, and I would have you try it still . . . We have sent you some ginseng" (Smith, Stout and Minkema, *Jonathan Edwards Reader,* p. 312).

Edwards also, surprisingly to some not familiar with Puritan views on such matters, recommends in true apostolic fashion "a little wine for her stomach's sake": "You may also try steeping it in wine, in good Madeira or claret; or if these wines are too harsh, then in some good white wine . . . And for a cordial take some spices steeped in some generous wine that suits your taste, and stomach" (Smith, Stout and Minkema, *Jonathan Edwards Reader,* pp. 312–313). Then comes some classic advice from those who perhaps, like the woman healed by Jesus, had "suffered at the hands of many doctors": "And I should think it best to pretty much throw by doctors, and be your own physician, hearkening to them that are used to your constitution" (Smith, Stout and Minkema, *Jonathan Edwards Reader,* p. 313). More homely medical advice follows. Then, at the end of a lengthy postscript, "The family all unites in their love to you" (Smith, Stout and Minkema, *Jonathan Edwards Reader,* p. 313).

I have a feeling that that single sentence might best express the tenor of the Edwards household.

WAYS TO MANAGE A HEALTHY FAMILY LIFE

How can we today encourage and apply some of these ideal lessons of the practical outworking of the principles of Scripture?

We might not want to go to the extreme of the Puritans in this matter: a Puritan preacher would have his children sit beneath the pulpit during his (probably lengthy) sermon, facing the congregation, so that their good behavior and attentiveness served as a witness that he as pastor was managing his household well! Nonetheless, Paul does say, "If anyone does not know how to manage his own family, how can he take care of God's church?" (1 Timothy 3:5). This does not mean that everyone in the family must personally profess faith, or (even) that every adult offspring must follow at least a morally respectable lifestyle. It means that the young family under the roof and rule of the parents must be visibly and clearly well organized, respectful, and generally an example of what the family of God is intended to be.

Many pastors would quake in their boots at such high expectations. There clearly are exceptions, though: children with problems of a special kind cannot be expected to sit still for lengthy periods of time. The world has altered and no-one expects children to remain still through an hour's lecture of an intellectual and complex sort. Still, in the non-Western world good behavior among children is more usual. We in the West may be pandering too much to our children.

Somehow this model of family life needs to come from exemplary Christian leaders. If Albert Schweitzer was right that "Example is not the main thing in influencing others. It is the only thing," then we need to construct examples of effective Christian ministry that speak to our need to develop healthy family lives. To have a personal family life of moral and spiritual chaos is a disqualification for Christian leadership. Perhaps we need to advance fewer people with sparkling gifts, and more of those with exemplary households.

CHANGING FAMILY PATTERNS

Starting well is important. Too frequently, pre-marital Christian relationships are the same as non-Christian dating. There is the same emotionally charged commitment, leading to hurt people after the break-up. There is the same sexually promiscuous activity, perhaps with some young Christians assuaging their conscience by being "technical virgins." We have come so far away from Edwards' day of 'courting' that a return to that practice is almost a challenge of mythical proportions. Perhaps, though, some return to this mode of behavior among singles is paramount. We might still want to call it "dating" ("courting" could sound archaic to some), but we need to give it a descriptive epithet, like "Christian dating." That is, we date when we are not sure we are going to marry someone and stop dating them when we are sure we are not going to marry them. Dating is our culture's formalized way of finding a spouse, but we do it in a Christian way. We do not get overly emotionally committed. We spend time in groups of people. We stay away from physical temptation.

In particular, though, we look for a spouse on the basis not of physical or emotional attractiveness, but of spiritual love for God. Such is the age-old wisdom of Proverbs 31:30:

> Charm is deceptive, and beauty is fleeting;
>   but a woman who fears the Lord is to be praised.

The same need to return to the application of biblical principles, not the unthinking aping of secular social standards, applies to nurturing the marital relationship once it has begun. Endless debates have raged about what it means for the man to be the "head" of the household. Nonetheless, Paul's practical challenge is clear: to be the head of the household means to live and die to self as the head of the church did. The model of husband leadership in the home is the model of the bleeding sacrifice of Christ at Calvary. Men in their marriages need to relearn that a healthy and harmonious relationship with their wife – as beautiful and treasured a thing as that is – comes at least at the cost of their personal inconvenience. We have to invest in and be self-sacrificial in this relationship. Only then are we a Christian (Christ-like) head of the household.

With regard to rearing children, the Bible is full of often-read but seldom-practiced principles. There is the need for discipline as well as, and as an expression of, love. There is the requirement that fathers get involved with the spiritual development of their children, which again requires sacrifice. But it brings great joy too. Jesus himself, in another context, said, "It is more blessed to give than to receive" (Acts 20:35). Sow much, and we reap much; sow little, and we reap little. This basic Christian discipleship lesson is applied acutely to the life of the family – we need to give of ourselves in order to receive for ourselves.

With all these high ideals, there is a need, in conclusion, for another biblical principle to be expressed: the principle of forgiveness, grace and the opportunity for a new start. There are rules to Christianity.

Paul, for instance, says of himself that he is "under Christ's law" (1 Corinthians 9:21). Yet the heart of the gospel is the offer of forgiveness to the repentant. We can keep God's rules only because of, and in the power of, grace. When we think of our need for the reconciliation of family and effective ministry, we turn then in repentance and faith to the great God of the universe and ask for his blessing, help and forgiveness and the power of the Holy Spirit to please him to his glory.

Christ himself invests in the success of family life. According to Ephesians 5, the marriage relationship is not only a natural ordinance for the blessing of individuals and society; it also has a message. It is a mystery revealed: "'For this reason a man will leave his father and mother and be united to his wife, and the two will become one flesh.' *This is a profound mystery – but I am talking about Christ and the church*" (Ephesians 5:31–32; my emphasis). Marriage is a message about Christ and the church. It was designed from the beginning (the quotation from Genesis ties the purpose to creation) to reveal the mystery of Christ. Ultimately, because of that, because we are talking about the message of Christ, successful and godly families matter and are possible. Christian marriage is a gospel proclamation.

THE EDWARDS MESSAGE

WHY LISTEN TO EDWARDS?

Jonathan Edwards lived a long time ago, and was not perfect like Jesus. Why should we listen to what Edwards said? Here are a few of the many reasons why we should pay attention to him.

Jesus gave Edwards to the church as one of its teachers: "It was he [that is, Christ] who gave some . . . to be pastors and teachers, to prepare God's people for works of service, so that the body of Christ may be built up" (Ephesians 4:11–12). Not everything Edwards said was right, so we cannot model our lives on Edwards without exception. Yet Edwards is a gift of the Lord Jesus Christ to build up his body, the church. If we are a part of the church, we will benefit from being attentive to Christ's teachers.

Edwards taught us how to respond to Enlightenment secularism, which in turn helps us understand how to interact with post-Enlightenment postmodernism. We must re-form the intellectual and cultural achievements of our age upon the foundation of God's Word. This requires understanding both the mind of the day and the mind of Christ. And it requires a solid personal commitment to change life our minds in accord with Jesus: "We take captive every thought to make it obedient to Christ" (2 Corinthians 10:5).

Edwards had eight insights or lessons that are especially instructive.

1. *He taught us how "revival is biblical" (see chapter 2).* This is a lesson in a true understanding of revival as God's premier means of advancing his kingdom. Revival is a gracious gift of God that may be sought through the means of prayer, repentance, anointed preaching, humility and evangelism. Perhaps our greatest need in the church is the rediscovery of a fully biblical notion of revival and a faithfully biblical practice of seeking revival.

2. *He taught us how "true experience of God is heart experience" (see chapter 3).* This is a lesson in rightly conceiving and therefore rightly receiving spiritual experience as both rational and emotional. Our tendency is to identify experience of God as either primarily logical or emotive; Edwards teaches us that true experience of God is 'heart' experience, meaning a combination of the soul's abilities to will, think and feel in encountering the living God.

3. *He showed us how to analyze new Christian movements by their "fruit" (see chapter 4).* This is a lesson in wisely discerning the wheat from the chaff of burgeoning new Christian movements. Edwards' principles are stringent but not legalistic or restrictive of the work of the Spirit. He does not "throw the baby out with the bathwater," but provides methods of establishing which is the "baby" and which the "bathwater," which help us to rescue the baby and throw out the bathwater.

4. *He identified the central problem of our humanistic age: it is insufficiently "God-centered" (see chapter 5).* This is a lesson in radically revolutionizing our whole thought structure around the complete sovereignty of God. Not only has God been removed from many areas of public debate, not only do many in secular society replace God with other central points of reference, like science or entertainment, but even in the church our view of God has been so tamed that his presence is rarely revolutionary and more often merely salutary. Edwards provides modes of thinking through world views that securely re-establish God's centrality.

5. *He modeled for us consistency to God's Word even in so-called "secondary matters," and explained how such secondary matters can sometimes have "primary importance" (see chapter 6).* This is a lesson in avoiding "dumbed-down" Christianity. While Edwards (as one of the forefathers of the modern evangelical movement) was clear about the importance of sticking to the main thing of the essentials of the gospel, he also realized that some non-essentials were taught in Scripture and therefore also needed to be obeyed. Furthermore, he understood that sometimes (not always) non-essentials have essential importance because of their function in the life of a person, church or historical situation. It is a call to stick to high-octane Christianity lest we lose the gospel itself in our search for ever simpler ways of repackaging the basics.

6. *He exemplified that "effective leadership must be biblically intelligent leadership" (see chapter 7).* This is a lesson not of the importance of being intelligent, but of the crucial need for Christian leaders to have their intellectual presuppositions formed by the mindset of the Bible. Edwards was astonishingly intelligent, but what most surprised contemporary observers was his thorough Bible-soaked approach to all matters. Much of Edwards' (and any) effective leadership is governed by our willingness to be biblically and not merely humanly intelligent.

7. *He had failings and so taught us that ultimately we must learn from God and look beyond man, for "human leaders fail" (see chapter 8).* This is a lesson in humility and the avoidance of idol worship. All branches of the church have a tendency to exalt human leaders to iconic proportions. Edwards failed in some significant ways, and we should not brush his failings under the carpet. But in a spirit of charity we should see them clearly. In so doing we become more conscious of our great God and his willingness to use even failures like Edwards, or you and me.

8. *Perhaps, most surprisingly, Edwards' progeny witness to the life of a good "family man" and thereby encourage us that "family life and effective ministry are reconcilable" (see chapter 9).* This is a lesson in the necessity of severe balance. I say "severe," for finding balance in

ministry these days requires strong determination to carve out time and space for our family to flourish. While the world exerts its pressures on family life, the church does too, with its increasing demands and decreasing resources. Edwards models for us a systematic commitment to raising godly children and nurturing a joyful marriage.

What would it mean to have an "Edwards-influenced life"? Should we be so defined by someone other than God? To have an Edwards-influenced life is to be pointed towards the source of all blessing, honor and glory: God himself. Edwards is a means (among others) for us to be drawn closer to Christ and find eternal peace and salvation in him. Christians are not ultimately to be defined by secondary epithets, such as "Baptist," "Presbyterian" or "Anglican." We can call only one person Master: Christ alone. To hear Edwards' message is to recognize and embrace that. We are not to be "Edwardeans" or followers of Jonathan Edwards, but followers of Christ and him alone. Edwards helps us do that in some unique ways.

WHAT WOULD THAT MEAN TODAY?

The Edwards message would create something like these portraits of an *individual,* a *church* and an *evangelistic mission.*

An Edwards-influenced individual

To follow Edwards would not mean wearing a wig (as Edwards did), nor would it mean riding a horse (as Edwards did), nor even necessarily preaching for an hour in the morning on Sunday, an hour in the evening, and another on Wednesday evening in a midweek lecture. In these matters, as in many others, it is important to follow the spirit, not the letter, of the law, to apply the principles or lessons that Edwards' message implies to contemporary or individual existence. It might not mean being a pastor, though Edwards was. It might well not mean being a missionary, though Edwards did that. An Edwards-influenced person could be someone who never wrote a book or preached a sermon, despite the fact that Edwards did a lot of both.

Edwards had his failings, so not everything he did can be copied unthinkingly. Yet the spirit of his character, the tenor of his ministry, is the one thoroughly devoted to the cause of Jesus. In essence, therefore, an Edwards-influenced individual (man or woman, child or adult) is someone carefully shaped after the pattern of Jesus Christ.

In particular, Edwards points us towards some uncomfortable challenges. In our contemporary world, "doctrine," or "the teaching of the Bible," is much despised, so in our churches doctrine is greatly watered down. One of the great challenges facing an Edwards-influenced individual is not to give in to the temptation to be an anything-goes doctrinal Christian.

Let me give one example. Sometimes as a pastor I come across Christians who have visited a wide range of churches in their spiritual journey. Occasionally I hear statements like "Jesus is the main thing," or "As long as they're talking about the cross I'm happy," or even "They had a Bible, so it must be biblical." These statements are evidences of shocking doctrinal ignorance among many (even "mature" Christian leaders). Of course, *Jesus is the main thing*, and the cross is the central issue of Christianity, and the authority of the Bible establishes our belief system soundly. But to equate these as adequate by lukewarm references to "Jesus" or "the cross" or having pew Bibles is to be simple-minded to the point of being prey to any wandering charlatan. No heretics or false Christian teachers come out and say they are *against* Jesus or the cross of the Bible, for no-one with a Christian conscience would be tempted by their message. These charlatans say they support Jesus; they are pious and pray and have Bibles nearby, but the Jesus they preach is a subtly different Jesus.

It is not only, though, the danger of heresy that an Edwards-influenced individual will be equipped to avoid. He or she will also be rescued from a myopic divisiveness about spiritual experience. Anyone who has engaged in any kind of missionary work will know it is empirically difficult to claim that no miracles are no longer more performed in the name of Jesus. These are not the "weeping Mary" false miracles of Roman Catholic medievalism. People are being healed. People are being helped. Muslims are coming to Christ through visions and dreams. It is difficult to escape this supernatural dimension to God's work in the world if we are familiar with non-Western Christian movements.

In the Western church, though, it is easy to fall into the trap of dismissing all claims to the miraculous as being tarred with the same brush as the wacky fringe. There *is* a wacky fringe, and being an Edwards-influenced individual will guard us from it. At the same time, however, being an Edwards-influenced individual will cause us – without embarrassment and with thorough doctrinal conviction – to seek experience of God (not experiences themselves) of the highest and most enthralling kind possible. We will aim to go on being "filled with the Spirit" (Ephesians 5:18); we will recognize we have not "already obtained all this" but will "press on towards the goal to win the prize for which God has called me heavenwards in Christ Jesus" (Philippians 3:12, 14).

Which brings up the most obvious challenge an Edwards-influenced life would bring to an individual: Edwards' eternal perspective. It breathes through his life. It is immanent in all his preaching. It is what makes secular scholarly analyses of Edwards fall very wide of the mark. Edwards plainly did not invest much capital or treasure in this life. He invested in heaven. And he warned of hell. At some point around the 1960s "heaven" and "hell" were dropped from the frequent proclamation of evangelical ministries, if not from their theoretical allegiance. Edwards was practical about heaven and hell. As we saw in the last chapter, in a letter to his daughter Esther he counseled her that her present sufferings were given her by God to teach her not to expect reward in this life, and so to put her hope in heaven. How different would the advice of most pastoral counselors have been today! We might have told her to trust in God, that it would work out for her good even if she could not see it. How many would have advised her to use this as an opportunity to learn the great lesson of life, that this life is preparation for the next?

To hear Edwards' message does not mean to be escapist from the challenges of this world, but to invest (Mightily! Energetically! Vigorously!)

while still here to reap dividends in heaven. We are to "lay up treasures" in heaven (Matthew 6:20) by following Christ faithfully throughout this life. It does, though, mean we have to change some of our habits as well as our basic perspective. We are the to think of ourselves as pilgrims not tourists. We are to sacrifice (by becoming a missionary or pastor or by tithing or by telling others about Jesus at work) for rewards in heaven. Not much of the New Testament makes any sense without a real and living hope in heaven. Unfortunately, the pressures of this instant commercialized world make us forget the ultimate destiny of our journey. As such, perhaps not much of the Bible does make sense.

Hell is a four-letter word, and many see it as offensive to use and proclaim it. Edwards, as we have already seen, did preach hell. He warned of the judgment to come. We often look at Edwards' plain speaking about the terrors of hell as distinctly distasteful and perhaps even starkly medieval, rather than crisply biblical. Edwards certainly employs shocking metaphor when he speaks of hell: but then so does Jesus, who warned of "hell, where 'their worm does not die, and the fire is not quenched'" (Mark 9:48; Jesus, quoting from Isaiah 66:24).

But do we believe in hell? If we do (and this is not the time to enter into an extensive biblical defense of its veracity), then no amount of warning could ever be enough. If I believe that those who reject Jesus Christ personally and redemptively are going to spend eternity in conscious torment, then how could I not warn people of "the wrath to come" (1 Thessalonians 1:10)? But we seem have moved away from a belief in the reality of hell. Or perhaps we just think people are less likely to come to church if we mention hell: we're scared of putting them off by "hellfire" preaching.

Again, though, the question is not one of copying Edwards' style and technique verbatim, but of imitating his heart and concern by tearfully and prayerfully rescuing sinners from judgment and bringing them to eternal joy and delight in God's presence.

Another aspect of the portrait of an Edwards-influenced individual would be a commitment to world missions. Edwards' biography of David Brainerd, as we have seen, influenced many pioneer missionaries. His vision went beyond the narrow confines of his immediate environment to the global harvest of God's kingdom. Edwards-influenced individuals will not be narrow denominationalists, nor see evangelism in terms of their own backyard only, but will catch the vision from Christ for the gospel to go to all nations.

There are many other components that would be formative for an Edwards-influenced individual. In general terms he or she would look much like a typical conservative (or "classic") evangelical, but with these provisos and challenges: there would be a greater commitment to doctrine, a properly biblical understanding of revival, a creative engagement with current intellectual culture and an evangelistic and missionary zeal. Edwards calls us to live out the principles of the gospel in practical life.

AN EDWARDS-INFLUENCED CHURCH

Once again, it is not necessary for an Edwards-influenced church to look or feel old-fashioned, for Edwards was at the cutting edge of the Christian movement. The Great Awakening broke many traditional boundaries of Christian ministry, but Edwards was its most lettered supporter. He did not spurn the novelties of Wesleyan hymn singing. George Whitefield himself, as we have seen (for all his shocking innovations for the religious conservatives), was invited to Edwards' pulpit.

However, perhaps what is most striking for a contemporary church seeking to be served by the teaching of Jonathan Edwards is not his willingness to be novel, but his determination to be orthodox. There is a balance here, of course, and, depending on where the church is, and what its culture, tradition and dominant voices are, there will be a tendency to lean either in an overly traditional or overly trendy direction. However, an Edwards-influenced church would be one that not only espouses the orthodox gospel of Jesus Christ, but that seeks to express that gospel in its structures and operations. This does not mean eternal navel-gazing in interminable business meetings; it means principled practicality, not pragmatic opportunism. Whereas there are things an Edwards-influenced church would not do (out of principle), there are other things an Edwards-influenced church would do (on the basis of conviction).

For instance, an Edwards-influenced church would *have a high regard for careful Bible teaching*. Some say Edwards was not an expository preacher, because his sermons did not go through a text of the Bible by chapter and verse. This is a mistake. Expository preaching is not a commitment to a certain mode of preaching (about 40 minutes with three points), but is a definite *philosophy* of preaching. That philosophy is the belief that in teaching the Bible carefully, God's voice is heard. It would be hard to find anyone with a greater the commitment to the philosophy of expository Bible teaching than Jonathan Edwards.

That said, Edwards' sermons were not (on the whole) especially intellectual. An Edwards-influenced church would certainly allot a significant portion of time in its services to Bible teaching. But an Edwards-influenced church would not necessarily be served up elite intellectual categories. A typical Edwards sermon is short on exposition and long on application. Most preachers today who claim to be "expository" feel this is a commitment to being the reverse. There is a need, they seem to feel, to speak at great length about the technicalities of the passage. However, an Edwards-influenced church, while embracing rigorous Bible teaching, would celebrate preaching that nourishes not just the mind (though it does that) but also the heart and soul.

Additionally, an Edwards-influenced church would *hold to a high view of membership*. Edwards' Communion Controversy was, in its most broad sense, a conflict about the nature of the church and its membership. Is the church a gathered community of the converted? Or is the church an institution of the local society, and therefore composed of genuine as well as nominal Christians? Through the history of the church there have been those who have stood on either side of the question. As we have seen, Edwards firmly endorsed the view that the church is a community of the redeemed. He also saw that this had implications with regard to membership. A member of the church must give a credible (in the judgment of charity) testimony to having received grace and having a personal faith in Jesus. In our day, too many churches have either no real membership or a membership that is merely theoretical and not connected either to the converted or even to the attending Christian. An Edwards-influenced church would not be overly hostile in its membership process, but it would insist that a real Christian is to be a member of a true local church and that a true local church is to be composed of (in the judgment of charity) genuine Christians.

More broadly, an Edwards-influenced church would *be a prayerful church.* As we saw earlier, Edwards pioneered the "concert of prayer" movement, whereby people from diverse Christian denominations are encouraged to join across the world on a particular day to cry out to God for revival. Because the Welsh revival of 1904 so emphasized prayer, and yet ran out of steam, leaving many empty chapels in its wake, some have reacted negatively to this desire to pray to God for revival. They fear it is passive: the "wait and see" attitude to evangelism rather than the "go and tell" instinct, which is more biblical. They also fear it can become imbalanced and remove the priority of preaching or Bible teaching from the life of the churches. However, none of these fears needs to be realized along with a firm commitment to passionate concerted prayer. An Edwards-influenced church would be a church frequently on its knees. It would not only have God talk to them through his Word; it would also make use of the means of grace of talking back to God in prayer – in all things making known their requests to God.

In addition (and perhaps, in priority order, no. 1), an Edwards-influenced church would be *an evangelistic church.* Methods of evangelism change as cultures change, and how they change is a missionary question. Ask any missionary (effective in a gospel ministry) and you will find that styles of outreach must change, dependent on the culture you are seeking to reach. Paul witnesses to this fact when he says that "I have become all things to all men so that by all possible means I might save some" (1 Corinthians 9:22). When Paul says he has become all things, he does not mean "all things without qualification." In fact he has just listed all the things he has in mind in the previous few verses – he became a Gentile to Gentiles, a Jew to Jews. This does not mean (Paul is careful to explain) he acts in an immoral or unbiblical way, for he is still under the law of Christ. It means that in matters now only *culturally* Jewish or Gentile, he is flexible.

There are some principles about evangelism that will always shape our evangelistic efforts. The gospel must be taught as well as caught. The gospel is a message and not just a lifestyle, and so for evangelism to take place there must be non-Christians present and the gospel proclaimed. Evangelism must also involve the church. To evangelize effectively means to bring someone from the world to the church; it is to perform a "transplant" operation, where an individual believes in the Christ and is thereby incorporated into the local body of Christ, the church. These (and other) things are not up for grabs: we are to evangelize lovingly, with truth and candor, not hidden agendas; with godliness, not in a manipulative or selfish way.

Nonetheless, while many doctrinal and principled matters of evangelism must *not* change, there are also some matters of evangelistic method that *must* change as we move from one epoch to another, or one from culture to another. Discerning which these are is not always easy, but an Edwards-influenced church will evangelistically impregnate the culture in which the church is immersed.

An Edwards-influenced evangelistic mission

An Edwards-influenced evangelistic mission may seem almost a contradiction in terms, for Edwards had a high view of the local church, and the modern-day non-church-based "parachurch" evangelistic organizations did not exist in Edwards' time. There were societies for the propagation of the gospel, and these are the grandfathers of the para-church evangelistic organizations. But organizations such as the Universities and Colleges Christian Fellowship, Campus Crusade, and many others, are far more recent additions to the Christian universe. How would Jonathan Edwards' distinctive theological vision shape these organizations? What would an Edwards-influenced Christian Union look like?

To begin with, Edwards' distinct piety would have a formative effect on any and all of our evangelistic missions. Too many of our missionary organizations, whether "foreign" or home mission, develop a piety almost exclusively geared up to getting results. There are too few quiet days, too little sense of the need for personal renewal, too little understanding of the worth of developing personal godliness through times of Bible study and prayer and reading, let alone meditation and reflection. Evangelistic missions tend to be beehives of work and generate a workaholic culture of piety, where godliness is equated to productivity. Edwards was highly productive, yet his personal notebooks and records of the inner life are laced with a desire not for more and more, or larger and larger, "ministries," but for God himself. Edwards is seeking him. Edwards' Resolutions are the best example of this attitude. Here are a few:

> 1. Resolved, that I will do whatsoever I think to be most to God's glory . . .

> 2. Resolved, to be continually endeavoring to find out some new invention and contrivance to promote the forementioned things.

> 3. Resolved, if ever I shall fall and grow dull, so as to neglect to keep any part of these Resolutions, to repent of all I can remember, when I come to myself again . . .

> 7. Resolved, never to do anything, which I should be afraid to, if it were the last hour of my life . . .

> 11. Resolved, when I think of any theorem in divinity to be solved, immediately to do what I can towards solving it, if circumstances don't hinder . . .

> 25. Resolved, to examine carefully, and constantly, what that one thing in me is, which causes me in the least to doubt of the love of God; and to direct all my forces against it . . .

> 40. Resolved, to inquire every night, before I go to bed, whether I have acted in the best way I possibly could, with respect to eating and drinking. Jan. 7, 1723. (E. Hickman [ed.], *The Works of Jonathan Edwards* [Banner of Truth], 1988, vol. 1, pp. xx–xxii)

And so the Resolutions continue: "69. Resolved, always to do that, which I shall wish I had done when I see others do it. Aug. 11, 1723."

To which we should add that Edwards also determined to "Remember to read over these Resolutions once a week." This kind of committed seeking after God would revolutionize many a Christian's life. It would also have a healthy effect on evangelistic missions in general, tending as they do to emphasize performance over piety.

In addition, an Edwards-influenced evangelistic mission would *not be separated from the ministry of the local church,* for Edwards had a high view of church. He could not have envisaged how someone claiming the to follow Christ could not be an active member of a local church. Many of our parachurch evangelistic mission organizations perhaps unconsciously encourage a situation in which meaningful involvement in local congregations is next to impossible. Given that situation, church discipline begins to break down and we have the condition we face today, when "Christians" can pass from one congregation to another, from one Christian parachurch mission organization to another, without ever having to face up to the challenges of living in close proximity to other Christians in community. Evangelistic missions, because of their busy schedules and frequent arrangement of conferences at weekends, inevitably discourage members of these evangelistic missions from taking an active role in church – they are just not available enough to do so.

An Edwards-influenced evangelistic mission would look far more like the model we find in Acts 13–14, where Paul and Barnabas are sent out by the local church at Antioch, go on evangelistic mission, and then return to the local church at the end of their pioneer ministry. They were always a part of the local church, commissioned by it and accountable to it. Nonetheless, they were "sent out" and "set apart" according to the calling of the Holy Spirit (Acts 13:2–3). Yet they also returned. Our foreign evangelistic missions most naturally emulate this model. Evangelistic mission organizations based more locally, though, need to have a constant cycle of being "sent" and then "returning" to the church for feeding, nurture, accountability and encouraging the church with reports of how God is using them to advance the gospel and grow the kingdom. So here are the three portraits of Edwards-influenced individuals, churches and evangelistic missions: each is to be modeled after the spirit of the gospel expressed by Edwards, not copying the historic idiosyncrasies of Edwards himself.

SOME BENEFITS

Learning about someone like Jonathan Edwards guards us from cultural and historical blind spots. Too often, our contemporary Christian scene is shorn of any historical sensibility. We are adrift in the immediate and the current, and so blown here and there by the latest Christian fad or fashion. Reading Edwards (among other historic great teachers of the Christian church) enables us to see where what we take for granted is worthy of criticism and therefore needs to change from a biblical point of view.

To hear Edwards means to *resist the temptation to dumb down church to an organization solely given over to marketing religion.* Edwards shows us that the New Testament not only teaches us the gospel, but also gives us principles of the gospel that apply to the structure of the church. In fact, we find, if we do not have those gospel principles expressed in our structures, it is likely that our churches – perhaps now successful – will in the next generation (if not before) become mere signposts of the importance of thoroughly obeying the Word of God. This is a call not to restrictive legalism, but to biblical faithfulness in worship and how we "do church."

To hear Edwards means *embracing a fully biblical understanding of revival.* Too many contemporary Christians read of revival and think of the crass showmanship and emotional manipulation of revivalists. We rightly eschew these underhand techniques. Revival, however, is the sovereign work of God in response to his stirring-up of means that he blesses with revival. We pray for revival; we seek revival with holiness, humility and faithful, radical, preaching of his Word. This is an understanding of revival that is not *just* "Keep on doing the same old thing and God, if he wants to, will blast us with revival." It is an understanding of revival by which, in conjunction with the normal means of well-organized and creative evangelistic efforts, we *also* deliberately and consciously pray and seek God for a revival anointing on and beyond our efforts.

To hear Edwards means *refusing to limit our horizons narrowly to this local geographical space in which God has placed us, but lifting our eyes and our energy towards the global harvest of the gospel.* Mission is not only home mission; it is also international mission. Edwards understood the essentiality of international mission to the heart of the gospel, and propagated it strategically though his biography of David Brainerd and his theology of revival sweeping throughout the world. To be Edwards-influenced means to pray for *and be involved with* the global harvest, by sending missionaries and having Christians from non-Western countries come and minister to us in the West.

To hear Edwards means to *develop a personal devotional life that is the intense, joyful and beyond the normal expectations of our paper-thin contemporary piety.* Edwards sought God in prayer, in hard work, in repentance, in faith; he longed for a deeper experience of God. We too commonly are satisfied with "having become a Christian," and then take our relationship with God for granted. To be Edwards-influenced means to seek God first and then his kingdom.

To hear Edwards means *avoiding iconic worship of Edwards himself, or any other human forebear, but accepting their testimony to God himself.* Edwards failed – great man as he was – in a number of ways. We too will fail. All our human heroes have failed. To be Edwards-influenced means *to be driven into the arms of Christ!* It means *following where Edwards led, to Jesus!* It does not mean a fascination with "the Puritans" for the sake of the historical or personal kudos that may gain us in some circles. *It means being fascinated with God and his Word!* Edwards, above all, was a man of the Bible, studying the Bible more than his contemporaries; to be Edwards-influenced means *likewise to find our ultimate source of information and teaching about God in the Scriptures,* while learning from Edwards and other teachers of the past and present about what the Bible says.

To hear Edwards means *to honor the institution of the family and, if married, to invest in our families as a primary arena for our godliness to be expressed.* Edwards gave time, effort and consideration to the spiritual development of his family. He did not look at them merely as extraneous baggage to his life but as a principal gift of God for him to nurture and develop, and for which he was responsible. Husbands, take note! Men in ministry, take note! We are married to our spouse, not to the church!

To be influenced by Edwards may mean *to have to face "strange providences" in our lives, unforeseen tragedies or surprises, and face them with confidence that God will bring good out of the situation.* Edwards' removal from his pulpit and banishment to the frontier town of Stockbridge could not have seemed more odd to the Christian world. What was God doing? In fact, though, while there, Edwards penned some of his most influential books. It was indeed a "strange providence," not an act of fate, and an Edwards-influenced individual will embrace apparently random, even vicious, occurrences with a confidence in the sovereignty and loving nature of the great God of the universe. To be Edwards-influenced *means to suffer, but not without cause!* It means to know that God, in his greatness, uses even our frailties and weaknesses for his glory, and it is to make the most of the time we have been given for that end and for that great purpose of glorifying the one true God of the universe.

To be influenced by Edwards means, above all, *to live a life of worship in which, instead of worshipping our work, working at our play, and playing at our worship, we radically and truly understand that the greatest experience and joy of life is found in God and him alone.*

To whom be all praise. Amen.

BIBLIOGRAPHY

The Works of Jonathan Edwards

All volumes published by Yale University Press, New Haven, CT.

Ramsey, P. (ed.), *Freedom of the Will*, vol. 1 (1957, 1985)

Smith, J. E. (ed.), *Religious Affections*, vol. 2 (1959, 1987)

Holbrook, C. A. (ed.), *Original Sin*, vol. 3 (1970)

Goen, C. C. (ed.), *The Great Awakening*, vol. 4 (1972)

Stein, S. J. (ed.), *Apocalyptic Writings*, vol. 5 (1977)

Anderson, W. E. (ed.), *Scientific and Philosophical Writings*, vol. 6 (1980)

Pettit, N. (ed.), *The Life of David Brainerd*, vol. 7 (1985)

Ramsey, P. (ed.), *The Ethical Writings*, vol. 8 (1989)

Wilson, J. F. (ed.), *A History of the Work of Redemption*, vol. 9 (1989)

Kimnach, W. H. (ed.), *Sermons and Discourses*, 1720–1723, vol. 10 (1992)

Anderson, W. E., Lowance, M. I. and Watters, D. (eds.), *Typological Writings*, vol. 11 (1993)

Hall, D. D. (ed.), *Ecclesiastical Writings*, vol. 12 (1994)

Schafer, T. A. (ed.), *The 'Miscellanies'*, a–500, vol. 13 (1994)

Minkema, K. P. (ed.), *Sermons and Discourses*, 1723–1729, vol. 14 (1996)

Stein, S. J. (ed.), *Notes on Scripture*, vol. 15 (1998)

Claghorn, G. S. (ed.), *Letters and Personal Writings*, vol. 16 (1998)

Valeri, M. (ed.), *Sermons and Discourses, 1730–1733*, vol. 17 (1999)

Chamberlain, A. (ed.), *The 'Miscellanies', 501–832*, vol. 18 (2000)

Lesser, M. X. (ed.), *Sermons and Discourses, 1734–1738*, vol. 19 (2001)

Plantinga Pauw, A. (ed.), *The 'Miscellanies', 833–1152*, vol. 20 (2002)

Lee, S. H. (ed.), *Writings on the Trinity, Grace and Faith*, vol. 21 (2003)

Stout, H. S., Hatch, N. O. and Farley, K. P. (eds.), *Sermons and Discourses, 1739–1742*, vol. 22 (2003)

Sweeney, D. A. (ed.), *The 'Miscellanies', 1153–1360*, vol. 23 (2004)

Other titles Bonhoeffer, D., *Life Together* (New York: Harper & Row, 1954)

Dodds, E., *Marriage to a Difficult Man* (Westminster, 1976)

Hickman E. (ed.), *The Works of Jonathan Edwards*, 2 vols. (Banner of Truth, 1988)

Kimnach, W. H., Minkema, K. P., and Sweeney, D. A. (eds.), *The Sermons of Jonathan Edwards: A Reader* (Yale University Press, 1999)

Marsden, G., *Jonathan Edwards* (Yale University Press, 2003)

McDermott, G., *Seeing God* (IVP, 1995)

McDonald, H. D., *Ideas of Revelation: An Historical Study, 1700–1860* (London, 1959)

Moody, J., *Authentic Spirituality* (Kingsway, 2000)

Moody, J., *Jonathan Edwards and the Enlightenment* (University Press of America, 2005)

Murray, I., *Jonathan Edwards* (Banner of Truth, 1992)

Smith, J. E., Stout, H. S., and Minkema, K. P. (eds.), *A Jonathan Edwards Reader* (Yale University Press, 1995)

STUDY GUIDE

Questions for Personal Application

CHAPTER 1: EDWARDS IN OUR TIMES

1. Can I think of some reasons why the study of Christian teachers from the past can provide useful perspective on spiritual questions today?

2. What is Jonathan Edwards' contribution, beyond a mere *"Sinners in the Hands of an Angry God"* caricature?

3. In what way am I influenced by the Enlightenment heritage, which its emphasis on rationalism and scientism? In what ways am I influenced by the post-Enlightenment contemporary culture, with its emphasis on relativism and subjectivity? How does Edwards' response to the Enlightenment help me find a more confident (less defensive) grasp of Scripture?

4. Am I satisfied with churches which have a very superficial level of Bible teaching, or are there ways I can encourage pastors and teachers to dig deep into God's Word?

5. What would Jonathan Edwards say if he walked into my church?

6. Why is it important to be willing to listen to what Edwards would say to our times?

CHAPTER 2:
REVIVAL IS BIBLICAL

1. When I hear the word 'revival' what do I think? Is that what Jonathan Edwards meant by revival? Is that what the Bible means by revival?

2. How, according to Jonathan Edwards, may we encourage revival in our midst?

3. What does the Bible teach about revival?

4. What can we do to revive preaching in our day?

5. What can we do to revive church in our day?

6. What can we do to foster a spiritual revival in our day?

CHAPTER 3:
TRUE EXPERIENCE OF GOD IS HEART EXPERIENCE

1. If someone tells me that God is telling them to do something, should I always assume they are right? How do I assess claims of the "God told me" kind biblically?

2. What is the heart of spiritual experience? Does this "sense of the heart" mean being really excited? Does it mean something more than that? What does it mean to not only feel, not only think, but *know* God? Is that "sense of heart" my personal experience? If not, what can I do about it? If it is, how can I praise God and encourage others to experience God in this way too?

3. How does this sense of the heart view of spiritual experience change my attitude to what I want to get out of a sermon? Or of a worship meeting?

4. What are the ways that I can encourage myself to grow in sensing God?

5. What does it mean to "see" God?

6. Does this help me steer a biblical course between rationalism on the one hand and emotionalism on the other?

CHAPTER 4:
WE NEED TO ANALYZE NEW CHRISTIAN MOVEMENTS BY THEIR FRUIT

1. Is it wrong to be judgmental? In what cases should we exercise our critical faculties? What is the difference between judgmentalism and being discerning?

2. What kind of doctrinal tests are useful to discern true from false spiritual movements? Do I feel sufficiently equipped to tell the difference between true Bible teaching and false religion? If not, what can I do to get more doctrinally aware?

3. Why are doctrinal tests a necessary but not a sufficient test of spiritual experience?

4. What are some "negative signs" that are commonly and mistakenly used to judge spiritual experiences today?

5. Which of the other six principles do you find most relevant to discerning in your situation?

6. Why is it more important to be able to apply these principles yourself rather than simply 'know the answer' in only one situation?

CHAPTER 5:
THE CAUSE OF MODERNISM'S PLIGHT
IS ITS MAN-CENTEREDNESS

1. Do you think there's anything wrong with our modern world? What do you think is the root cause of the problems of our age?

2. How is it that our human freedom can be sustained only by God's sovereignty? In whose service is perfect freedom? Do I submit to God in my life – or do I fear he's out to get me?

3. Why does God-centered preaching allow for more practical and helpful application?

4. Is God genuinely in the center of my life? Do I pay lip service to God or life service?

5. What would a God centered world, church, family be like? Is that what my church or my family is like?

6. What is the key beginning step to becoming more God-centered?

CHAPTER 6:
SECONDARY ISSUES SOMETIMES
HAVE PRIMARY IMPORTANCE

1. Is the church today selling the gospel or telling the gospel? How can I faithfully tell the gospel?

2. Why did Jonathan Edwards think the issues around the "Communion Controversy" were so important?

3. Are there any 'secondary' issues today in our lives which, because of their associations, are becoming matters of primary importance? What would those issues be? How can we deal with them?

4. Are there churches today that accept non-regenerate members? Does this matter? If so, why?

5. Is it possible to construct such a palatable atmosphere that church is dumbed-down to the point of no longer being different from a social club? Are our churches like that?

6. Would I be willing to stand against, even at personal cost, an issue that would negatively influence church culture or Christian witness?

CHAPTER 7:
EFFECTIVE LEADERSHIP MUST BE BIBLICALLY INTELLIGENT LEADERSHIP

1. Is there a difference between intelligence and biblical intelligence? How can I make sure I have the latter?

2. What are the three principles of biblical intelligence? How do they help answer current criticism of biblical orthodoxy?

3. What are some areas today where principles of biblical intelligence need be applied? What about in my life – are there areas of "guidance" where biblical wisdom (the "fear of the Lord is the beginning of wisdom") need speak?

4. Does it matter if our pastoral leadership becomes modeled after administrative leadership in the non-profit or business world? Are there distinctives of pastoral leadership which need pertain (2 Timothy 4:2)?

5. Am I growing in my understanding of the Bible? What habits can I begin to generate today which will help me understand the Bible better?

6. Is there a need for biblically intelligent leadership in the secular world? How would I exercise such discernment in a leadership position in a non-religious environment?

CHAPTER 8:
HUMAN LEADERS FAIL

1. Is there an area in my life which is undermining the credibility of my Christian confession?

2. Am I in a genuine and regular accountability relationship with a mature believer?

3. Do I hold Christian leaders in idolatrous view, like religious rock stars, or do I esteem them and submit to their biblical leadership as patterned after the New Testament?

4. Have I failed in my life? Is there a road back (John 21:15-19)?

5. What might be some of the blind spots in our contemporary Christian culture that subsequent generations will puzzle over? Does the Bible speak clearly about some issue which conservative Christian culture ignores?

6. If I am in a position of pastoral responsibility, how can I exercise care in proactive pastoral work?

CHAPTER 9:
FAMILY LIFE AND CHRISTIAN MINISTRY ARE NOT IRRECONCILABLE

1. Many statistics record the increasing pressures on pastoral ministry: if I am a pastor am I aware of these contemporary pressures? If I am not a pastor, are there ways that I can alleviate some of these pressures on my pastor?

2. Edwards had a busy ministry schedule, as well as a large family. Granted, he had support structures, including servants, that most of us do not enjoy. Yet Edwards combined some practical principles of balancing family life with ministry which are exemplary. What were some of those principles? How can I apply them to my personal life?

3. Jonathan and Sarah Edwards' marriage is famous for its health. What were some of the secrets of their successful relationship? If I am married, in what ways can I incorporate similar modes of behavior and attitudes of heart?

4. If I have children, and am in ministry, are there ways that I can involve my children in my actual regular ministry? If I don't, can I encourage my pastor to so integrate his family into his ministry visits, for instance?

5. If I am a father, can I get more involved in the spiritual development of my children? How so?

6. Does the example of Sarah Edwards, and her influence down through the years, encourage me if I am a wife or mother?

CHAPTER 10:
THE EDWARDS MESSAGE

1. Can you summarize the eight lessons or insights that Edwards provides (page 170-172)?

2. Is it appropriate for Bible believing Christians to seek to be "Edwards-influenced"? In what way?

3. What would an Edwards-influenced individual be like? Could I be more committed to the significance of firm and secure doctrinal convictions?

4. What would an Edwards-influenced church be like? Could my church become more committed to solid Bible teaching?

5. What would an Edwards-influenced evangelistic mission be like? Could my local Christian university group, or parachurch outreach organization, become more self-consciously a mission of the local church?

6. Am I persuaded of the need to develop a life where all my joy and blessing is found in God and God alone?

Printed in the United States
76059LV00005B/427-450